need to know?

Scrapbooking

Yvonne Worth

Collins

First published in 2007 by Collins
an imprint of
HarperCollins Publishers
77-85 Fulham Palace Road
London W6 8JB

www.collins.co.uk

Collins is a registered trademark of
HarperCollins Publishers Limited

10 09 08 07
6 5 4 3 2 1

A catalogue record for this book is available from
the British Library.

Yvonne Worth asserts her moral right to be identified as
the author of this work.

Project editor: Guy Croton
Editor: Vanessa Townsend
Designer: David Etherington
Series design: Mark Thomson
Photographer: Tim Sandall
Front cover photograph: Marie-Louise Avery
Back cover photographs: Tim Sandall/Marie-Louise Avery

ISBN-13: 978 0 00 723174 4
ISBN-10: 0 00 723174 1

Colour reproduction by C(   )ursan, Singapore
Printed and bound by Prir   by Exp
Hong Kong

Contents

What is scrapbooking?

Scrapbooking is fast becoming one of the best-loved of all hobbies. It is so appealing because it offers a delightful way of preserving your most cherished memories. With a little imagination anyone can produce exciting scrapbook pages and albums, ranging from the fantastically fun to the deeply dramatic.

must know

Scrapbooking offers a great opportunity for you to organize all those photographs which have been tucked away in boxes or drawers and cupboards for years. Set aside some peaceful, quiet time, find somewhere you can spread out, put on some of your favourite music and allow yourself to indulge in a nostalgic trip back through time, reliving a few special memories.

The essence of scrapbooking

A scrapbook is essentially a creative way of preserving and presenting your treasured photos to protect them from deterioration and damage, allowing them to be enjoyed by present and future generations alike. The added attractions of scrapbooking are that it allows you to use any tools, techniques, materials, memorabilia, skills and scraps available to you; it also gives you the chance to develop your own individual style and even the opportunity to experiment with new ideas. Basically, when it comes to 'scrapping', anything goes; just allow your creativity to flow and your artistic inspiration to guide you and you can't possibly go wrong!

What's on a page?

The final form that your scrapbooking page takes is essentially up to you; however, there are a few key elements that commonly appear on most designs. Your photo (or photos) will usually be the focal point of your design, although there may be occasions when this is not the case. If you choose, it is perfectly valid for you to use your skills to create magnificent projects that are filled with souvenirs, memorabilia and embellishments, without a photo in sight.

You will quickly learn how to turn familiar photos into fun and highly personalized scrapbook pages.

Titling is an essential element of any page and can take the form of either one word or an entire phrase that encapsulates something of the tone and subject matter therein. Titles can be big or small and positioned anywhere you choose. They can be handwritten, computer generated, stencilled or stickered.

Personal notes – known collectively as 'journalling' – are other important elements on scrapbook pages. They can range from simple annotations, dates and captions added to your photos, to blocks of text that tell the story of your page or reflect the subject matter itself. In short, this is your opportunity to express yourself and to allow your personality to shine through.

Scrapbook pages can be anything you wish them to be. Remember, you are in control - at liberty to add whatever you choose or feel inspired to include in your design.

Embellishments or accessories are items added to your layout for decoration, although they may also be souvenirs or cherished pieces of memorabilia.

This book introduces you to a variety of techniques designed to inspire, including making mosaics (pages 82, 122), stained glass effects (pages 124-5), and the special effects demonstrated in projects such as 'Animal Magic' (pages 76-7) and 'Taxi' (pages 88-9). You will also be shown paper crafts such as weaving and layering (pages 110-11), pop ups (pages 114-17), building blocks (pages 148-9) and optical illusions (pages 150-1).

Acid-free and archival quality paper

Nowadays, most products aimed at the scrapbooker are of 'archival' quality - basically, materials that are made to last and protect. Look for paper and card, page protectors, adhesives, albums and other products that are marked 'lignin-free' (lignin is an acidic substance found in wood pulp and fibre), 'acid-free', 'archival quality' or 'buffered' (paper). Excess acidity causes photos and paper to discolour and turn brittle. A pH of less than 7.0 is considered 'acid'. You can invest in a special pen to test paper acidity levels and special sprays that can help neutralize products which are overly acidic (see pages 187–8 for suppliers' websites).

Albums and altered books

Scrapbooking pages are usually made into albums that are organized by theme, subject or event. Give your album consistency by planning a beginning, middle and ending, just like any story book; or use a colour or a particular design feature throughout to create unity.

When you become a more advanced 'scrapper', you might like to venture into the exciting world of 'altered books'. This artform is similar to scrapbooking, in that you can use any techniques or materials you wish. However, instead of creating pages and filling albums, you use an extant printed book as your base, cutting and colouring and adding photos and numerous embellishments to create a unique work of art.

There are hundreds of scrapbooking websites, many of which have online chat rooms, noticeboards and 'galleries' where you can share ideas or just enjoy looking at other people's creations (see pages 186–8).

1 The basics

You've made the decision to become a scrapbooker: this is where the real fun begins! It's best to start off by being as organized as possible, so make sure you have the materials you need in front of you before you begin. As this delightful hobby becomes more and more popular, there is an ever-growing variety of albums, cardstock, paper, accessories, tools, embellishments, inks and pens available to the 'scrapper'. This chapter will start you off on your scrapbooking adventure by showing you the type of equipment you will need at this stage to get you going on the basics.

Tools and materials

As with any new hobby, you will need to invest a certain amount of money at the outset. However, before you start splashing out on items that you may not need or ever use, first take stock of what you have at home. You can then sensibly decide what other basic items you may need to get you started.

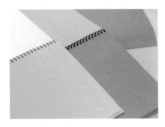

Spiral-bound albums (above) are ideal for newcomers to scrapbooking. You can move on to themed, shop-bought albums as you progress (see below).

Scrapbooking essentials

As a beginner, it is best to start small with a few basics and to invest in more costly items and equipment only as you grow in confidence and wish to develop your techniques or learn to experiment with new ones.

The essentials you will need for any scrapbooking project are photos, an album or cardstock to make the pages, a small selection of coloured papers for matting and decoration, some ready-cut shapes or stickers and rub-down lettering or photo-safe markers or pens, pencils, a paper trimmer (either a

Ring-bound albums (right) are useful for adding pages to later on.

As a more experienced scrapbooker, you can even create your own album covers.

Having the right tools - such as a selection of scissors and craft knives, as shown here - is integral to the quality of your work.

mini guillotine or a craft-knife and cutting mat), a pair of sharp scissors and some photo-safe adhesive.

The most basic type of scrapbook is a simple spiral-bound version or stapled variety. Others include: ring-bound (see page 12), post-bound (held with removable bolts or post screws), strap style (plastic straps hold pages or page protectors in place), and sprung spine (the spine itself opens up to grip your pages).

The market is flooded with papers and products aimed at the scrapbooker, but before you start shopping, take a look at what you already have at home - you may be surprised by the many useful items to which you have access. For example, decorative scissors allow you to create interesting design effects with papers and photos, but you may come across long-forgotten dressmakers' pinking shears tucked away in a drawer, which can be used for exactly this purpose.

Remember, successful and pleasing scrapbook designs are not dependent upon expensive or complex tools and materials: indeed, some of the most stunning layouts are extraordinarily simple and straightforward, and are often crafted from the most basic of materials.

must know

The more advanced scrapbooker may prefer to create their own handmade papers, album pages and covers (see above). For novice scrapbookers or those more interested in working on the actual pages rather than creating their own albums, there are plenty of ready-made options available from stationery shops or the web (see pages 187-8).

Paper and cardstock

Paper and card is available in a range of sizes, colours, thicknesses and textures. Paper is sold by weight, in grams, which will be marked on the packaging or labelled on the shelf if sold in individual sheets in a shop. When scrapbooking, you will normally use lightweight card for your pages (100–120g is usually sufficient). The more robust varieties of papers (around 160g) will be used for your decorations, particularly if you are making cutout shapes or photo mats (background mounts in coloured card or paper on which photos or other items are placed to highlight or give emphasis to your photo). However, experiment with different weights and find what works best for you and your requirements – some of the heavier papers can be difficult to work with, while the more delicate papers can be too fragile.

Paper and card can be bought in single sheets or in packs. Some companies even offer mixed or starter packs of card and paper. These can be reasonably priced and are useful if you are just starting out in scrapbooking (see pages 187–8 or visit any good stationery or craft store).

A variety of different papers – patterned, plain or painted – is used here to create a very individualistic layout.

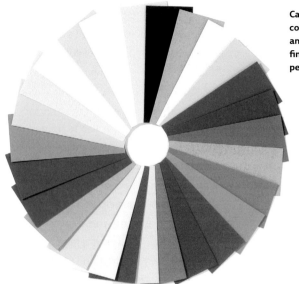

Card and paper is available as plain, coloured, patterned and textured and in a range of different surface finishes – glossy, matte, metallic, pearlized or embossed.

There are some stunning speciality papers on the market, including animal markings, Indian prints, silk and linen weaves, metallic and holographic finishes.

Glues and adhesives

Types of adhesives range from liquids, sticks, mounts, tapes and strips (single- and double-sided) to glue dots (in different sizes – usually regular and micro). Repositional or removable tape and glue is now readily available and, although it is a little more costly, it is very useful, as it allows you to change your mind and make adjustments, even after you have fixed item(s) to your page. However, after a time some types do set and will become permanent.

You will almost certainly end up using a variety of different adhesives for different jobs; for example, double-sided tape is extremely useful for affixing photos neatly to your page, while glue dots are invaluable for attaching gems and small accessories. However, after a little while you will probably find that you develop a preference for working with particular types of glue in different situations.

Whichever type of adhesive you decide upon, look for 'photo-safe' or 'acid-free' varieties, as these will not damage your photographs.

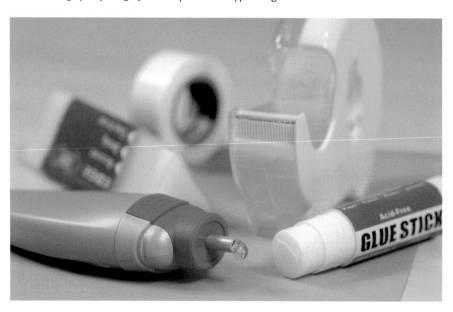

Stencils and templates

Commercial stencils and templates are usually made from thin sheets of plastic or metal and allow you to reproduce shapes and patterns accurately. They are available as simple geometric shapes, letters, patterns and border designs, as well as more complex and detailed designs for the advanced stenciller.

Stencils can be used for cutting photographs into shapes, creating frames and mats for your photos and making paper shapes, decorative borders or corners. Journalling stencils allow you to draw regular lines (straight or shaped) onto your layout to use as guides for hand-drawn decorations, lettering or journalling (see page 7). You can even make your own stencil by cutting out designs from card or thin plastic.

When using stencils or templates, you will also need a well-sharpened pencil and a pair of small, sharp scissors or a craft knife.

Stencils are invaluable scrapbooking tools and are available in a variety of shapes and sizes.

Hand-held or table-top punches are easy to use and create great shapes and cutouts.

Punches and die cuts

Punches are plastic and metal templates used for pressing out shapes; they are a favourite tool of many scrapbookers. These devices come in hundreds of different patterns, producing fabulous shapes from paper or card quickly and easily. Lovely effects can be achieved with even one or two simple punches used creatively (see below). Use medium- to lightweight papers, rather than heavier varieties, which are more difficult to manipulate for the beginner. For more information on punches, see pages 106–9.

A single punched-out flower shape is used to good effect in the 'I Love Daisy' project on pages 100–1.

Die cuts are pre-cut paper shapes that are cut from a special die cutting machine. You can find die cuts in any number of different shapes, patterns and colours either in craft shops or on the internet.

Pens, pencils and crayons

Pens are vital scrapbooking tools. There are all sorts of pens available from stationery or craft stores, from simple fine-tip pens to more decorative varieties such as double-ended, dotting, calligraphy, scroll, chisel and brush pens. Look for pigment pens, as these are usually colourfast and waterproof. They can be found in dozens of colours and inks (including gel, glue and glitter or metallic pens). As you go along you will be able to experiment and discover the types of pens and tips that work best for you. However, even if you are not interested in decorative hand lettering or drawing, you will still find a basic black pigment pen to be an invaluable addition to your scrapbooking toolbox, if only for marking up or for outlining purposes.

Pencils and crayons are also useful scrapbooking items – even the simplest drawing or the most delicate shading can give your layout a delightfully individual touch. Watercolour pencils, which are similar to regular pencils, can be used either dry or dipped into water. They offer extra flexibility when combined with a dampened brush to create a subtle, watercolour effect.

Chalks, paints and inks

Paints, inks and chalks can be fun to use. With practice, you can quickly master the art of manipulating these materials to create your own colourful backgrounds, or to shade or highlight cut or torn paper edges, or colour-punched shapes and lettering.

Pens, markers, pencils, paints, crayons, chalks and other pigments need to be acid-free, fade-resistant, photo-safe and, where possible, waterproof.

Getting organized

You may start scrapbooking with only a few tools and supplies, but you will be amazed at how fast your collection will grow. Establish a system for storing your tools, materials and photos so that you can find them quickly and easily when you need them.

Craft bags and tool belts are particularly useful for people who have limited space and do not enjoy the luxury of a dedicated scrapbooking workspace.

Caring for your tools and supplies

From the outset, it is a good idea to organize and take proper care of your tools and materials. Keep all your scrapbooking tools together, as this way you will not waste valuable time searching for an elusive tool that you need for a particular job.

Arrange all your tools into distinct groups, such as 'pens and pencils', 'punches', 'glues', 'scissors and knives' and 'templates and stencils'. Put aside any that are broken, duplicated or unwanted and either fix them, get rid of them or swap them with other scrapbooking friends.

Make sure that all your tools are clean before you put them away. Carefully remove any traces of ink, glue or dirt from scissors, craft knives and scalpels. If any of your punches have become blunt, sharpen them by punching through kitchen foil or fine sandpaper; if they are sticking, punch through wax paper a few times in order to free them up. Test pens and markers and discard any that are no longer working; make sure that all pen caps are tightly in place.

Storage

Store your items in labelled containers that are easily accessible and which will keep them clean, dry and free from dust.

Paper products

Separate out full sheets of paper from scraps and arrange them in order of colour. Pull out patterned papers or card and sort them by either colour or theme, whichever you prefer. Do the same with die cuts, punched pieces and stickers.

Memorabilia

Souvenirs and memorabilia should also be stored in protective boxes or binders. Sort them by event or theme and place individual items in acid-free bags for protection. If your photographs, in particular, are not stored in acid-free sleeves, they will eventually start to disintegrate or fade badly – they can always be left in the protective sleeves and attached to your layout. If you do not want to use the original photo or fragile item, take a scan or photograph and use the photographic image of the item(s) on your layout instead (see page 66).

See-through plastic storage containers are particularly useful, as they keep your items clean and allow you to find exactly what you are looking for.

Organizing your photographs

The chances are that you have years' worth of photos and snaps hidden away in various places. If so, it is a good idea to consolidate all your photographs into one integrated system so that when you come to start future projects you will find it much easier to locate the images you want and to make the most valid choices.

Find yourself a clear, clean space to work on and come up with some categories for sorting your photos into. For example, you might choose to sort them by year, by family member, activity or event; alternatively, by season, theme, subject or even colour scheme might work well. It is entirely up to you: you just need to work out which system will be the easiest, most useful and inspiring for you to use. Allow yourself a 'miscellaneous' box as well, for any

Choose photo-safe (acid- or lignin-free) storage boxes or folders (see pages 8–9). Find somewhere cool, dry, dark and as dust-free as possible in which to store your photo boxes.

photos which you are unsure about categorizing at this stage. Remember, there is no right or wrong way to organize your photos – you simply need to choose the way that works best for you and keeps you feeling motivated and enthused.

Making notes

As you sort your photos, jot down any thoughts, ideas or memories you have about the different images. You can keep a notebook or journal for this purpose, or write on sticky notes that you can then attach to the back of the photograph. You can even write on the back of the photo (some people like to write peoples' names or dates on photographs), but only use photo-safe pencils to avoid damaging the print. Alternatively, you might prefer to record your thoughts and ideas on a mobile phone, dictaphone or other portable device.

Inferior photos and duplicates

Scrapbookers inevitably have differing views on duplicates and inferior or damaged photos and whether simply to dispose of them or not. As a newcomer to scrapbooking, it is a good idea to hang onto them at first, as they are very useful for you to practise your techniques with or to cut for use as decorations. Also, you will be surprised at how effective even an inferior photo can be if it is improved with a little creative wizardry. However, as you progress and become a more confident scrapbooker, beware of hoarding unusable photos unnecessarily.

If you still hold the negatives of your prints, store them separately. This way, in the event of any damage occuring to your photos, you can make extra copies using the safely retained negatives.

must know

Both digital and regular photos can be backed-up on CDs. With proper care and if kept in the right environment, these will be safe for years. Store your disks in hard jewel cases rather than in soft plastic sleeves, as the latter can stick to the surface of your CDs if they are exposed to humidity or heat. Store disks away from direct sunlight, dust and extreme temperature change.

An introduction to colour

Good colour choice is fundamental to creating a design that is both interesting and pleasing to look at. There are certain basic guidelines to follow which can make selecting a beautiful colour scheme really easy.

Understanding colour

In traditional colour theory, red, yellow and blue are known as the 'primary colours'. They are so named because they are not produced by mixing other colours. All other colours bar black, white and grey are derived from mixing the primary colours together in different combinations.

Secondary colours are made by mixing proportions of two primary colours (for example, red + blue = violet; yellow + blue = green). Tertiary colours are made by mixing a primary colour with a secondary colour – for example, blue + green = blue-green (or turquoise). Neutral colours are considered to be white, black and grey. The tint or shade of any colour can be altered by mixing it with white or black. Adding white creates a lighter version, or tint, of the original colour, while adding black creates a darker version, or shade.

Using a colour wheel

Combining colours is largely a matter of individual taste and preference. Some people have a natural flair for colour and instinctively create the most wonderful combinations. A colour wheel can also help in combining different colours.

Essentially, a colour wheel is made up of the colour spectrum (think of the colours of the

This example both combines harmonious colours and features a background which picks up the colour from the toddler's clothes.

rainbow) placed side by side in a circle, from red to violet, as demonstrated in the illustration below.

Complementary colours are those directly opposite each other in the wheel: selecting these in combination can add a dynamic, exciting feel to your design. Colours that are next to each other on the wheel are closely related and considered to work harmoniously together. You might decide in favour of using only a single colour (monotone) and even experimenting with it by using it in a variety of tints or shades.

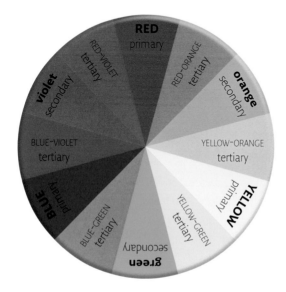

Colour wheels are readily available on the internet, from arts suppliers, craft shops and hobby stores.

Choosing your subject

Choosing a particular theme or subject for your scrapbooking page can be an excellent starting point for any project (whether this is a single design or a whole album). All your decisions for your design – such as colour scheme, decoration and accessories – can then be related to that topic.

Where to start

If you do not already have a particular photo (or photos) in mind that you would like to use, you might like to choose a specific topic that appeals to you instead. You can then look through your collection and pull out photos relevant to this topic.

Deciding upon a particular topic gives you an immediate direction in which to work, in the form of colour or embellishments. The beach or seaside, for example, suggests using yellows and blues for your colour scheme to reflect the sun, sea, sand and sky.

If you have already chosen your photo but are unclear about a theme, then take a close look at your photo and see what subject – or subjects – the content implies (the picture opposite of two playful children is perfect for a 'Fun in the Sun' layout).

Let your photo guide you

Give yourself time to examine your photo. Pictures contain a great deal of information that can give you invaluable clues as to how to proceed with your design: you just need to learn to pick up on those clues. Some questions to ask that will help you are: what range of colours is contained within the picture? Are the tones bright or muted? Is the picture itself light or dark? Does it feel warm or cold in quality? What is the mood? Is it happy or sad, upbeat or reflective? Is the photo background itself 'busy' and cluttered (lots of people or objects) or relatively simple (an empty beach, for example)?

Try to make design choices that are in keeping with the colour content of the photo itself. Gentle, muted images will often work well on a pastel or more subtle background, while dramatic, eye-catching images usually look good on a bright background. Equally, choosing a background colour in a contrasting shade can make your picture really stand out. Patterned backgrounds can be effective against photos that contain more solid areas of colour, but can be confusing to the eye where the background within the photo itself is packed with detail.

Although there is very little yellow in this picture, choosing bright yellow as a background colour works perfectly against the blue of the sea.

The faintly patterned, green background used here lends a tropical feel to this holiday layout.

Colour sense

In some instances, there will be colour choices you can make that will be useful in your design as they directly imply that particular event or theme. For example, an old photo taken on Christmas morning may not contain any red or green, but choosing a colour scheme based on these classic Christmas colours will automatically complement the image and give it a festive feel (see page 24). Similarly, choosing rich greens and browns to complement images of a tropical holiday (see opposite) will convey the desired impression. So, once you have decided on your theme, decide whether there are any obviously complementary colours or colour combinations that you could include in your design.

Developing a theme

As well as using your photos for inspiration, you can also allow the type of paper you have available to guide you, rather than the photo itself. It could even become the main focus of the layout – particularly if you have some interesting or unusual patterned papers in your collection or enjoy playing with colours and paper design. For example, a picture of your little nephew at the zoo can look fabulous against a gorgeous tiger-print background.

There may be occasions when you feel unsure how to use a particular theme, or are stuck on how to proceed, or find that you are repeating yourself over and over again in your scrapbooking projects. When this happens, as previously mentioned, let your photo or chosen subject dictate how your theme actually unfolds. For example, instead of choosing water as the theme for your seaside scene, why not use a child's bucket and spade, a sand castle, or even a beach umbrella as the focal point for your design? Equally, you do not need to limit yourself to elements that actually appear in the photo or photos that you are planning to use in your layout, as long as they make sense to the design you are trying to achieve. For example, you could easily choose a cake or decorative candles as the theme for a birthday party spread, even if there is not a cake in sight in any of your child's birthday pictures.

Your colour inspiration can be as simple as 'blue for a boy'!

watch out!

Remember: light-coloured images will not show up well against light backgrounds (or dark images against dark colours). Choosing a darker background for a lighter photo will help it stand out, as will a lighter background for a darker photo.

Choosing which photos to use

As a rough guide, you can normally use between one and six photos in any scrapbooking layout, although it is really up to you and, naturally, depends also on the particular techniques you are using and the effect you wish to achieve.

watch out!

If you have photos that are irreplaceable, don't let this prevent you from using these images in your albums. If you have a scanner and printer, make your own copies. If you don't, simply take them to your local copy shop.

Selecting your images

Once you have experimented with individual photos and different background papers, you can begin to move on and think about including more than one photo in your design. Remember, the aim is to keep things simple, so avoid going overboard and pulling out dozens of photos to use on a single page. If you are basing a design on a particular event, person or occasion and find that you have lots of different photos to choose from, separate them into different piles, choosing whichever groupings are the most meaningful to help you decide.

Using sequences of photos

You can also look for sequences of shots within your collection or similar shots of the same subject that were taken at roughly the same time, as these can make very inspired scrapbooking layouts. If you do have several similar shots then there is no need to choose the best – even if one or two are markedly better than the others; including several shots can add action to your design. The overall effect will be to create a slight impression of movement or action, quite literally showing a passage of time, even if only of a few seconds' duration. Incidentally, this is also a useful technique to try if you had intended to use only one image, but could not decide which shot to choose!

Random choice

To challenge yourself, why not just close your eyes and pick out a photo at random from your collection? Or, as an exercise, you might even try pulling out three or four random photographs and seeing if you can find a way to make them work within a single design. Start by asking yourself the questions raised on pages 26–7 and see if you can find any way of linking all or any of them together into one design.

This 'story effect' takes us through a mini 'emotional journey', giving us a brief glimpse of the baby's changing facial expressions just as he starts to cry.

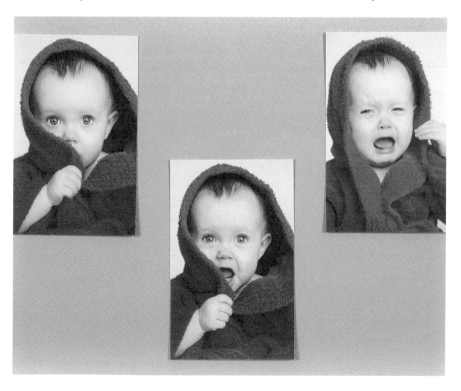

Using repeated images

Another technique that is very simple but which can be surprisingly effective in a scrapbooking layout is to use exact duplicates of the same photograph. Again, if you have a scanner and a printer you can quickly and easily run off a number of copies; if not, get them copied at your local copy shop or have duplicates made when you get your film developed.

Experiment with using duplicates of an image that is particularly meaningful or powerful to you.

Simply by using identical copies of the same photo, and just repeating the same image multiple times without cropping or changing the image in any way, is an easy and incredibly effective way of adding dramatic interest to your page.

These three crops of the same picture are identical in size, but give the dramatic effect of 'zooming in' on the little girl as she plays her instrument.

Equally, you could use enlarged or reduced versions of the image, which would give you the opportunity to try out different sizes of the same image and see what effects you can create. Move them around your page and look at different combinations. You might even try overlapping the images and see what happens.

Photo cropping

Alternatively, by cutting or shaping your photo you can even use different 'crops' of the same image to change the focus or draw attention to a specific element in the photograph (see the girl playing the violin, opposite, as well as pages 66–71 for a more detailed look at cropping).

You can also play with cropping your photos into different shapes and sizes – for example, circles, squares, triangles or rectangles – and arranging the shapes on your page. You could even try cropping your photos into themed shapes, such as droplets of water for rainy day pictures or simple leaves or flowers for forest walks. Alternatively, how about stars for your child's first theatre performance?

Be patient

At this stage you really don't need to be in any hurry to stick anything down. This is the time for you to keep trying out different ideas and to experiment with the photos and materials in your collection and discover what really appeals to you. If you want to keep a record of your results or wish to chart your progress (maybe for use in a future scrapbook?), don't forget that you can always photograph your work in progress.

want to know more?
- Using colour 42–3
- Adding texture 44–7
- Mounting photos 48–9
- Techniques for extra effects 60–3
- Cropping 66–71
- Improving your designs 56–9
- Scanning and printing 164–5

weblinks
- beginnersguide.com/arts-crafts
- learn2scrapbook.com
- mommychat.com/scrapbooking
- scrapbooking.about.com
- stencil-library.com
- tollitandharvey.co.uk

2 Simple layouts

Remember, when it comes to creating scrapbooking pages, there is no right or wrong way. The whole purpose of making them is for you to find ways of telling your own story and letting your personality shine through your projects. As you grow in confidence and master new techniques, your style will naturally develop. However, you will always create your best work when you are enjoying what you are doing, so with every project look for some aspect – no matter how simple – that you find fun and interesting, to inspire you.

Designing a basic layout

The word 'layout' refers to the arrangement of photographs, lettering, illustrations and embellishments. Scrapbooking layouts can either fit on a single page or spread over two facing pages.

Planning your page

Your photographs themselves will usually be the main focus of any scrapbooking page and the success of your design will also be greatly affected by your choice of colour scheme (see pages 42-3). However, of equal importance is the layout or arrangement of your page or spread (double-page).

A good design needs a strong focal point: this could be a photo, but it could equally be some other eye-catching element such as the title (a word or phrase used as a headline) to your page or an unusual embellishment or illustration.

Successful designs need to be well-balanced – a large photo could be off-set by several smaller elements in the opposite section. Make sure that your design is not top heavy (lots of strong images at the top of your page and very little at the bottom, for example), or weighted to one side or the other. In the case of double-page layouts, try experimenting by mirroring the designs on the left and right-hand pages to give balance to the overall layout.

Choosing your page size

Scrapbooking pages can be any size you choose, particularly if you are custom-making a page to frame and hang on the wall, or are creating your own album from scratch. However, many scrapbookers prefer to use commercially bought albums (see page 13) and the size and shape of album you select will then dictate the exact proportions of your designs for that album. Scrapbook suppliers are becoming more and more adventurous and the choice is growing fast.

Divide into grids

A simple but useful design technique to get you started and give balance to your composition is to divide your page into quarters or thirds and to use this as an invisible grid for your design, arranging the different elements of your layout within the various segments. To the right are examples of pages divided up into various grid systems. From top to bottom: in vertical quarters; even quarters; horizontal thirds; and vertical thirds. The scrapbook page below is a finished example of the grid in vertical thirds which is shown at the bottom of the page.

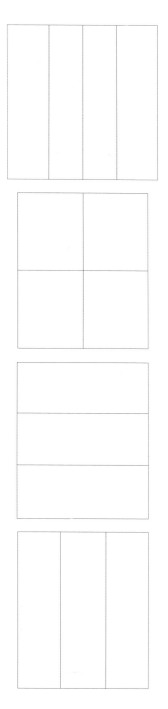

watch out!
Some projects will fall into place quickly, while others may take a lot more thought and effort. Don't give up – it's almost always worth persevering, but if you are really struggling, put the project to one side, take a break and come back to it later.

Choosing your design

Once you have chosen your page size and photo(s), try moving the photos around the page until you find an arrangement that looks balanced and which you are happy with. Gradually add in other items, adjusting the photos if necessary to maintain the balance of your design.

Avoid overcrowding

There are no rules as to how many or how few photos to use in your design, but avoid overcrowding your page, as this can make your design look cluttered. If you have a number of photos you wish to use on a spread, try using a single large portrait on one half of your layout and then group other related photos together on the other half.

Don't be afraid to leave blank areas in your layouts as this gives your design what is known as 'breathing space'. Basically, this means that less is more for some layouts (see left). Allowing space also prevents the various elements from competing with each other and prevents your layout looking messy. However, do try to make sure that space is evenly spread throughout your design, as this too will help give your composition a well-balanced feel.

Rather than overloading this page with embellishments, using only three main elements gives it just the right impact.

Fit in with the photo

A large, stunning landscape photo or beautiful portrait might work extremely well as a sole focus for your page. Similarly, some straightforward, lesser-quality snapshots will be less striking when used individually, but if put together in a simple grouping they may work magnificently.

This page is based on the design below (top left of the layouts), using a tag (see page 53) instead of a photo in the top right corner and carrying the title on from the top to the bottom.

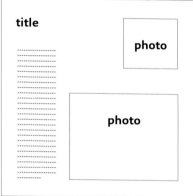

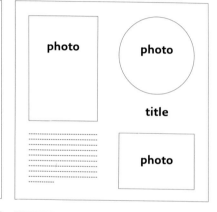

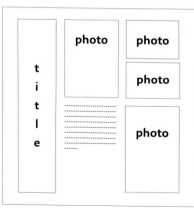

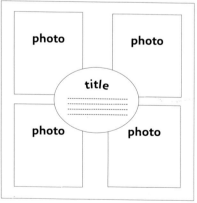

These are a few ideas for some basic single-page designs. Make sketches of any layout designs that you favour as these can be useful to refer to for future scrapbooking ideas.

Extra touches

Using a mixture of large and small images or objects
in your layout adds movement and interest to your
design. This is true, also, of photos that are alike:
using an enlargement next to a smaller version of a
similar image creates a very powerful effect. The
exact number of photographs that you will be able to
fit onto your layout will depend partly upon the size
of your scrapbooking page but also on whether you
are cropping any of your photos (see pages 68-9),
and whether you are overlapping any images.

To give your design a more casual feel, try tilting
one or more of the photos, but beware of arbitrarily
angling photos in different directions, as this will
look awkward and confusing to the eye.

Titling your design

Whatever form your page title takes (see box [above
left], pages 7 and 50-1) – whether it is ready-made,
hand-drawn, computer generated or made up of
cutouts, stencils, stickers, ink stamps or buttons – it
is essential that you choose a prominent position for
it. Make sure that it is clear and easy to read, to allow
it to stand out and enhance the overall effect of your
design. Indeed, sometimes the title itself can provide
the main focus for your page, instead of an image.
The actual wording you select for your title will give
some indication of the subject of your layout. It can
be a single word or a whole sentence, serious or light-
hearted, reflective or just plain silly – it's entirely up to
you. If no obvious title springs to mind, take a close
look at the photos and see if there is anything that
you might have overlooked that could inspire you, or
simply give your imagination free reign!

This layout features a tilted
image, adding a pleasingly
informal feel, as well as a fancy
title made up of lettered buttons
(see pages 100-1).

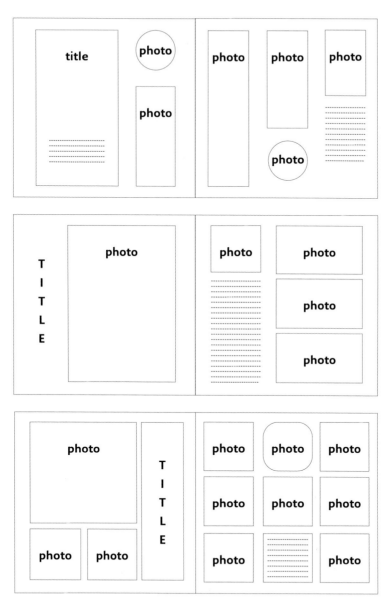

These double-page layout designs are all based
on a grid system that divides the page into thirds
(see page 37), here using a combination of both
horizontal and vertical divisions.

Using colour in your layouts

Colour is all around us, and it's probably for that reason that most people haven't thought much about it since experimenting with watercolour paints at school. There are some basic guidelines, however, that can help you in your scrapbooking.

Colour choice

As mentioned in the introduction to colour in Chapter 1, colour choice is crucial – even the simplest design can be utterly breathtaking with a thoughtful and inspired use of colour. Colour choice, however, is always a matter of personal taste.

Using a specific colour can accentuate or draw attention to certain aspects of your design (such as matching the blue sky or other colours that appear in your chosen photo/s).

Opting for complementary colours in your design (see pages 24–5) can instantly add an element of excitement or drama to your layout.

Getting warmer... getting colder

There are two main colour categories: warm (red, orange, yellow) and cool (blue, purple, green). Warm colours suggest excitement and are associated with the elements of earth and fire, while cool colours are more calming and are associated with air and water (or even ice). Colour has a profound emotional effect and can be highly atmospheric – choose a colour scheme which is consistent with the mood you want to produce, such as energizing oranges or gentle, relaxing greens (see pages 24–5).

Taking inspiration for your background design
from the colours (or patterns) in photographs
can be extremely effective.

Adding texture

Using only flat, solid colours in your designs can, of course, allow you to create stunning layouts. However, there is an ever-increasing trend in scrapbooking for adding texture in various forms in order to make pages more interesting.

Even the simplest item can add a special touch to your layout, but make sure that it is in keeping with the subject matter or colour scheme of your project.

One lump or two?

There are various ways of introducing texture into your layouts. These include: adding corrugated card or crumpled or distressed paper, speciality paper, card, fabrics or textiles with raised or textured finishes, applying textured paint, affixing small objects such as mesh, glitter, sand, seeds, buttons, ribbons, shells or even pebbles. See pages 73, 101, 116–17, 138–9 and 175 for examples of how to use some of these materials.

However, if you like the idea of adding texture but don't want to deal with lumpy items that could make your pages difficult to protect, then it's best to

Glitter is a delightful way to add sparkle to your layout. It can be stuck directly onto items of your layout (see pages 114–17) or used as the filling for 'shaker boxes' (see pages 132–5 and 174–5).

stick to using printed patterns and decorations to enhance your designs instead of the real thing.

Ready-made textures

Papers and cardstock are now available in a seemingly infinite array of different patterns and designs. Some printed papers carry photographs of subjects such as floral-print fabrics, paint effects and finishes, and images of nature such as leaves, sand or grasses. These types of papers are invaluable to the scrapbooker, both because they are so much simpler to work with than the original finish, and because they offer an easy and efficient way of adding pleasing textural effects to your layout without requiring any special skills, techniques or tools to manipulate them.

must know

Adding shadows to aspects of your design (by either digitally enhancing your photos or adding paper shadows to your page) gives your page the illusion of depth. A similar effect can be achieved by inserting foam spacers under one or more elements to raise them off the page and give them the appearance of being slightly three-dimensional (see pages 89, 130–1 and 150–1).

Paper crimpers come in a variety of sizes and provide a simple but effective way of adding texture and effects to papers and paper decorations.

watch out!

Remember to check that any paper or card is acid- or lignin-free, especially if it is going to be in direct contact with any photos. If you have papers that you are unsure about, you can buy a special pen that will allow you to test the acidity of your paper.

Decorative items

Pre-printed trompe l'oeil-style accents and embellishments offer a practical alternative to using the original articles on your layout, as these 'fake' decorations give you the opportunity of visually enhancing your design without adding unnecessary bulk or weight to your page. Ready-made die cuts (see page 19) of shells, buttons, ribbons, metal hinges, stones and leaves are just a few of the options that are currently available and can look just as good on your layout as the real thing.

Paper patterns

Even if you usually prefer using solid colours in your scrapbooking layouts, there will be occasions when introducing patterned backgrounds or highlights will be well worth the effort. Here are some guidelines to get you started on using patterned papers to add texture to your layouts.

Try combining one patterned paper with a plain paper in a co-ordinating colour (preferably one that appears in the pattern). To add texture, choose a paper that has a special finish, or crumple it into a ball then flatten it out (or iron it on a low heat to flatten it further). Alternatively, 'distress' the paper by gently rubbing the flattened surface with wire wool.

When using different patterns together, try combining dark patterns with light ones and mix large patterns with smaller ones (using only a small amount of the larger pattern to prevent it from dominating your layout). Where possible, choose patterns that are in co-ordinating colours and which have the same degree of brightness or intensity (this is referred to as the 'value' of the colour). You can also try combining patterns that are similar in style – elegant, geometric, whimsical, faux finish, subtle.

Decorative papers can be found in a variety of stylish patterns. Those used here really enhance the autumnal theme of this layout.

Mounting your photos

Matting or mounting your photographs refers to the technique of placing photos onto a background card or paper. Photos can be mounted directly onto your background or first mounted onto individual mats that are then attached to your page.

Using matting

Mats can be narrow or wide, single (made up of one paper) or multiple (made up of two or more papers, often in different colours – double or triple mounts being the most common) and should complement your photos in terms of colour, theme or mood.

Matting individual photos creates borders or frames that can enhance your photos. Matting also

MY FAVOURITE COAT

...JUST GOING OUT TO CHECK IF IT'S RAINING YET!

A simple layout that shows how effective matting an individual photo can be. The mat and background paper pick out the pink and yellow from the raincoat.

adds contrast and colour, drawing attention to a photo or series of images that might otherwise disappear into the background.

Mats can be cut or cropped to the same shape as your photograph or varied in shape for a slightly different effect. For example, try using an oval mount with a rectangular photo, or vice versa. Selecting a wider mount gives you the option of using the extra space for journalling directly onto the mat or enhancing your mats with hand-drawn decorations, stickers, punched shapes or other accents.

See-through corner mounts are designed to keep precious photos both fully visible and perfectly intact.

Temporary mounting

Corner mounts, whether invisible or decorative, offer a non-permanent method of displaying your photos. This means that you have the option of removing or replacing these photos at a later stage if you wish. These mounts are like tiny paper or plastic pockets that are self adhesive, so they can be easily stuck directly onto your page or mat. The corners of your photo are then inserted into each of the pockets.

Permanent mounting

There are a range of adhesives that will permanently fix your photo onto your mat or page. The easiest of these are probably mounting squares and photo splits. These are tiny squares of double-sided tape that come in a special dispenser. There are also mounting strips, regular double-sided tape and tape rollers. These adhesives are applied directly to the reverse side of all four corners of your photo. For extra secure fixing, add a little adhesive to the centre of the photo as well. Avoid using liquid glues with photographs, as these can cause them to buckle.

Choosing lettering

For some scrapbookers, lettering plays a major part in their layouts. There are many ways of creating lettering for your pages, including computer-printed titles and captions, cutout letters, rub-downs, ready-to-use stick-ons, rubber stamps and stencils and, of course, good old-fashioned handwriting!

must know

Occasionally, there can be some confusion between the words 'typeface' and 'font'. Increasingly they are being used to mean the same thing (a style of lettering). Strictly speaking, 'font' is the name given to a lettering style or 'family' (such as 'Times' or 'Arial'), while 'typeface' refers to the variations within that group (such as Bold, Italic, Narrow, Condensed, Oblique, Outline, Extra and even upper and lower case).

Words and phrases

Lettering can add a special something to your scrapbook design. The wording can take the form of single words, phrases or paragraphs, providing a title to your page or reflecting upon the content, either as individual captions to go with each picture or blocks of text. Wording can be small or large, simple or flowery; it can be discreet or provide the focal point to your page; it can state the obvious or have a meaning that only you understand – it's entirely up to you.

The rule of three

As a basic rule, the same advice applies to fonts as to colours, which is that in general it is best to use no more than three fonts on any one page. You can even stick to using just one font, or style, and varying the look by using a bolder, larger or heavier styling for the title with a regular, lighter or even italic version for your captions or journalling. For best effect, titles should be larger than text or captions.

Heavily decorative styles should only be used for titles or short phrases – simpler serif (which have little 'tails' at the end of each stroke) or even sans-serif fonts (straight edges and no 'tails') are easier to read and are a better choice for running text.

Lettering styles

If you own a computer and printer, creating lettering can be easy and fun, and you are virtually guaranteed successful results every time (see pages 168–9). However, when using computer fonts or when handlettering, always choose a style that is in keeping with the tone of your page, whether it is down-to-earth, sophisticated and elegant, formal or just crazy.

Plain (sans serif):

Happy days

Happy days

Happy days

Happy days

HAPPY DAYS

Plain (serif):

Happy days

Happy days

HAPPY DAYS

HAPPY DAYS

HAPPY DAYS

HAPPY DAYS

Elegant:

Happy days

Happy days

Happy days

Happy days

Typewriter:

Happy days

Happy days

Happy days

Handwritten:

Happy days

Happy days

Happy days

Happy days

Happy days

Decorative:

HAPPY DAYS

Happy days

HAPPY DAYS

HAPPY DAYS

Funky:

Happy days

Happy days

Happy Days

Happy days

Happy days

Happy days

happy days

happy days

Happy days

Happy days

Happy days

Happy days

Happy days

HAPPY DAYS

H A P P Y

H A P P Y

Accessories

Accessories or embellishments are the finishing touches that can make your layout look really special and are sometimes quite literally the icing on the cake (see pages 156–7)!

watch out!

Check that any accessories or embellishments you use are acid-free to ensure that they will not damage your photos. If you are at all uncertain, mount them on acid-free paper or card, or place them into protective pockets or holders.

Adding accessories

Any kind of embellishment can be used in scrapbooking – postage stamps, feathers, airline tickets, buttons, stickers, stamps, pieces of fabric, lace, pressed flowers, paper shapes, wire shapes, metal hinges, beads, tags, rubber stamps and more. See pages 187–8 for suppliers on the internet.

However, when adding decorative accents to your pages, bear in mind that they need to enhance the rest of your page and not overpower it or pull focus away from the photos. Be sparing with any ornamental touches and limit yourself to one or two per page, unless the subject matter justifies using more, of course. Too many extra items will quickly make your page look cramped and cluttered, so if in any doubt, less is more. Experiment with the final arrangement of any accessories before you actually stick them down, as you may find that when you put them on the page they have a very different effect to the one you expected.

Colour co-ordinate

Make sure that all items you have chosen are in perfect keeping with your chosen colour scheme. Even if you have found a sticker, stamp or bow that seems perfect for your design, if the colouring isn't quite right, don't use it!

Wooden beads
Simple materials are perfect for creating a more natural feel.

Coloured beads
Beads can be threaded into strings or glued down to provide texture.

Gems and sequins
Sparkly highlights can be added to create an element of fun.

Tags
Tiny or large, plain or fancy tags are used for labelling or decoration.

Gels
Colourful gels can make your page look good enough to eat!

Ribbons and bows
Ribbon can add a dash of elegance or fun to any page.

Buttons and fasteners
Buttons, keychains and decorative paperclips can all be used to enhance your pages.

Rubber stamps
Stamping is ideal for creating simple details or even backgrounds and border designs.

Stencils
Use stencilled shapes, letters and numbers to make cutouts for titling your pages.

Decorative scissors
Enhance photos, mats, mounts and borders by giving them patterned edges.

Paper shapes
Template shapes can transform backgrounds, mats or photos into something extra special.

Wax seals
For that ultimate touch of sophistication, wax seals are just the thing.

Accessories can add both texture and
colour to your page and can range from specially
purchased items to simple, everyday objects.

Improving your designs

Including simple paper shapes in your scrapbooking layouts is an effective way of enhancing your designs and adding variation to your pages.

Stencils, templates and rulers

As previously mentioned, there are ready-cut paper shapes in every possible colour, shape, size and style, as well as a vast array of commercially produced stencils and templates (see page 17). There are rulers and decorative scissors with patterned edges (such as scallop and zigzag) to help you create the perfect finish (see pages 12–13). However, although these can provide excellent additions to your scrapbooking palette, you do not need to rely solely on shop-bought tools and materials to produce top-quality scrapbooking designs. Sometimes the simplest techniques can create the most wonderful results (see opposite). Any new skill, though – however basic – requires practice, a little thought and a great deal of patience, so don't worry if you are not able to master the technique immediately or come up with the exact results you want first time.

Paper play

Adorning your pages with hand-made shapes gives you the freedom to choose designs that are both ideal for your project and totally unique in style. You also have the option of either creating your own template to reproduce one particular shape or working freehand to create original shapes that are all slightly different. There is also the added benefit

1 To make your own template, carefully mark out your design on a piece of card. If you want to use a torn-edge finish rather than cut edges (see pages 58 and 62), choose a bold shape with simple details, as it is much harder to tear intricate or complex shapes successfully.

2 Use sharp scissors or a craft knife, cut out your shape and make your template. Next, flip the card over and, holding it firmly in place, carefully draw around your new template onto the reverse side of your paper. This eliminates any risk of pencil marks on your finished item.

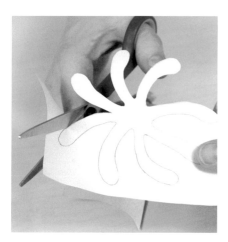

3 Following your pencilled pattern, cut out your paper shape. Take your time and avoid making longer cuts than you can comfortably control. If necessary, rest your arms on a hard surface to steady your hands.

4 Check your finished item and neaten up any untidy edges. Use your template to make as many copies of the shape as you need. To make your shapes even more striking, add some extra decoration (see page 117).

of requiring only the simplest tools – pencil, scissors and a ruler – or, in the case of torn edges, none at all.

Making your first shapes

Freehand shapes can be quick and easy to produce. Firstly you need to decide what shape you are going to make and then the kind of finish you want – do you want cut or torn edges or do you perhaps want to use a mixture of both?

Practise, practise, practise

To begin, practise on pieces of scrap paper and card. Anything will do, as this is an opportunity for you to develop your technique and experiment with papers and card of different finishes, textures and weights to see what effects you can achieve, so the more variation, the better. Don't waste good paper, just use what's around you – newspapers,

For a torn-edge effect, use a standard or decorative ruler to tear your paper against, draw a pencil line to use as a guide or, once you have more confidence, try working completely freehand.

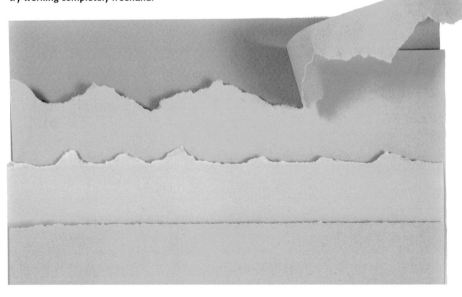

magazines, circulars, food cartons, toothpaste boxes, old envelopes or even unwanted photos.

Once you are ready to start working on your actual project, it is best to give yourself a pattern to follow in order to make your task as simple and stress-free as possible. However random the shape you wish to produce, either make a template first or use a pencil to draw out your design on the back of your paper. You can then either cut or tear the shape as you choose, using your drawn shape as a rough guide. This will prevent you from making unnecessary errors and wasting good paper.

Simple paper shapes can be pieced together in creative ways to build new images.

Shape shifting

Templates are useful, even if you don't follow them exactly. To create variations to designs, mark out your shape and then cut or tear inside or outside the lines, or alter the shape slightly to your requirement. For a more exact finish, use a pencil to mark out the changes to your pattern first.

Paper piecing

To create different effects, shapes can be used on their own or grouped together. This can either be done in layers (see left, for example) or with shapes pieced together to make another image, such as a flower. This can be made with four or more heart shapes placed together in a ring with the bases pointing in towards the centre and a little circle carefully placed to create the flower middle (see top right).

Adding variations

For further variation, make the same shapes in different sizes, colours or paper finishes.

Techniques for extra effects

Making the most of everyday items such as string, corrugated card, brown paper, sand paper or newspaper are inexpensive, easy ways to transform your designs. To top it off, a little well-planned hand lettering and some simple hand-made decorations can make your page look simply sensational.

Everyday items

Simple, everyday papers and products can look great on your page, whether used just as they are or coloured or altered in some way. However, products of this type will probably need to be treated first, as they are unlikely to be acid-free and may deteriorate and cause damage to any photos they are in direct contact with. As mentioned on page 46, test paper and card with an acid-testing pen, then treat with special sealant sprays, which are available on the internet or in craft shops, to seal the surface and reduce acidity.

String or thread can be used to hang tags and attach embellishments to your page and can be coloured to match your scheme. Alternatively, wind it into shapes to create titling or lettering (see layout, left). Draw your letters first and stick the string over the top using liquid glue. Otherwise, experiment with different types of wire, bending it into letters, numbers or shapes.

Hand lettering, easy as ABC

Hand-drawn letters and details can look fabulous, but unfortunately many people are put off by the idea of having to write or draw by hand. There is no need to avoid using hand lettering. Your writing style is something personal to you and therefore unique.

Working by hand gives you the freedom to write directly onto your page, in whatever shape and style you choose – you can also layer your letters by going over them in other colours or shades (start with the lightest and build up to the darkest), or decorate them with dots, flowers or hearts.

Hand drawing or lettering might give you your biggest thrill – putting those personal, finishing touches to your page and seeing it really come alive. However, having created a perfect page, if you fear ruining it with messy, uneven penmanship, here are some simple pointers that can help you.

Use writing grids

Using a ruler (decorative or straight edged), stencil or journalling template, pencil faint grids onto your paper. Lines can be straight, zigzag, wavy, curved or spiral and can be positioned horizontally, vertically or diagonally. Using the grids as guides will keep your lettering neat and even. You can also draw in an extra line to mark the position of the top of your capital

Your own handwriting can really personalize your layout, whether used for titling or journalling.

must know

When handwriting for your scrapbook, work slowly, using single, downward strokes where possible. Lift your pen after each stroke, even if the effect you are trying to achieve is a handwritten-script style, in which the letters are joined together. Using separate strokes will give you much more control and help prevent shaking hands.

The edges of corrugated card can be torn, or the surface of the card can be 'distressed' by ripping back the top layer to expose the corrugations.

1 To create symmetrical shapes, fold your paper in half so the reverse side is showing. Using a template, ruler or working freehand, draw one half of your design onto the paper, taking the fold as the centreline of your design.

2 Keeping the paper folded, gently tear out the shape, keeping a firm grip on the paper and working towards yourself for maximum control. The pencil lines are for guidance only, so do not worry about being overly precise.

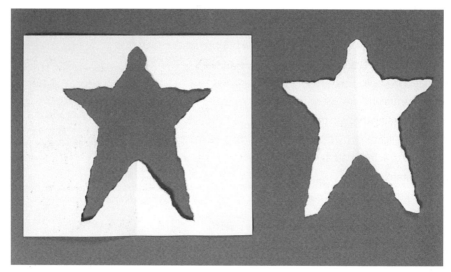

3 Tearing carefully (or cutting, if you want neater edges) will prevent the 'discarded' paper (above, left) from being damaged and gives you the option of using both the positive and negative shapes in your layout (see pages 178–9).

letters and another at the mid-way mark for the top of your lowercase letters. When you have finished, gently rub away the pencil guides. You can even pencil your lettering and then ink over the top. If you are using transparent ink, rub away your pencil guide first, little by little as you write, otherwise it will be sealed into your page and will be visible through the ink.

Test sketching

Sketch your wording onto tracing paper first. This will allow you to check that your text fits properly and will also show you how the finished article will look.

Tracing technique

Using a suitably easy-to-copy font, type up your text and print it to the required size, shape and format onto a piece of plain white paper. Place a piece of vellum (a speciality, transparent paper – also not as porous as other papers) over the top and trace your text onto it (see also page 139). Cut your vellum to size and fix it to your page. If you are using regular-finish paper, place the paper over a lightbox, so that the light shining through from underneath will allow you to see your printed wording through the paper. (If you don't have access to a lightbox, try taping both pieces of paper to a window to achieve the same result.) This technique is not suitable for heavier, more opaque papers.

Torn shapes

Create quick and easy accents for your page by tearing simple shapes (see left). These can be symmetrical or not, as you choose. Don't worry if your finished items are not exactly the same: slight variations will add to their charm.

want to know more?
- Introduction to colour 20–1
- Choosing your subject 26–9
- Paper folding 94–7
- Journalling 136–7
- Creating timelines 138–9
- Project ideas 140–1

weblinks
- 3scrapateers.com
- happyscrapper.co.uk
- momscape.com/ scrapbooking
- scrapbooksmag.com
- scrapbookbarn.com

The Halloween project on pages 176–9 is a good example of how to use torn shapes.

3 Working with photographs

One of the joys of working with photographs is realizing that the images you select need not be perfect to start with. You will quickly learn that you can easily alter and improve them by hand using simple but astonishingly effective methods. Over time you may even find that your scrapbooking experience starts to influence your photography itself, affecting the choices that you make when taking photos. Many of the techniques described in this chapter can also be applied to crafting paper and paper shapes, as well.

Cropping

Photographs can be cropped (trimmed or cut) with a craft knife, paper guillotine or scissors to improve the composition of your photograph by removing excess background, extra people or objects. You can trim photos to size or even alter their shape.

Copy before cutting

Before cropping any photo, if it is valuable or irreplaceable, a work of art or you no longer have the negative (or digital image), copy it first. In fact, it is advisable to keep the original intact and work with the duplicated version instead. With older, black and white – or even sepia – photographs, where possible always take a copy (especially if the negative no longer exists).

When making copies of photographs, it is best to make a colour copy, even if the original is black-and-white. You will get much better results, as colour copying will pick up and retain the range of tones and subtle variations in hue that would be lost in a straight black-and-white version.

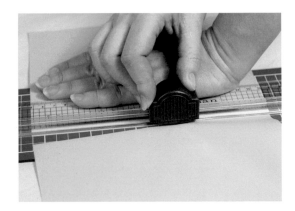

Guillotines are perfect for cutting neat, straight edges. Practise on scrap paper and unwanted photos to get used to exactly how much pressure you need to apply.

Mini guillotines

Although you can use scissors to trim your photos, mini guillotines are much easier to use. They are available in a range of styles and sizes from stationery and craft stores (see also pages 187–8) and are probably the easiest way to cut neat, straight edges. They have the added advantage of being safe for children to use, too (although an adult should always be present when any cutting tools are being used).

When operating a guillotine, hold your paper firmly against the paper guide, if there is one, or ensure that it is lined up squarely and held in place on your cutting mat if your model does not have a guide. It is usually preferable to work towards yourself, as this will give you the most control. Work steadily and evenly as you cut – jerky movements will risk your paper becoming skewed and your edges will be left jagged and untidy.

Craft knives and cutting mats

Craft knives (or scalpels) are another option for cropping and trimming. They are used in conjunction with special cutting mats, known as 'self-healing' mats, as the surface appears to mend itself as you cut,

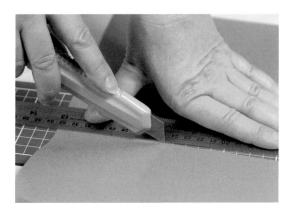

Craft knives and scalpels can be used for cutting lines of any shape and are particularly useful for cutting inner frames and sections out of the middle of photographs.

Cropping photos allows you to improve the composition of your photographs by getting rid of excess space, extra items or unwanted people.

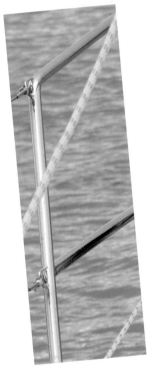

allowing you to keep on cutting without your blade catching in nicks in the mat's surface (see pages 187–8 for internet suppliers). Cutting mats are usually marked with a square grid pattern for you to use to help keep your photo (or paper) lined up properly as you cut and ensure you achieve an even finish.

Decorative scissors

Decorative scissors from a stationery or craft store can be used to create patterned edges on photos, mats, borders or even paper embellishments. Blade patterns range from simple zigzags to more complex designs. Some scissors can be flipped over to give a slightly different cut.

Patterned cutting can take a little practice to master. For a more even finish, as you cut, try holding the scissors in one position and turning the paper or photo. Use strokes that are as long as possible, realigning the blades with the stopping point of your unfinished pattern each time.

Remove to improve

Cropping can improve your images by removing unwanted items and areas, or even errors (however, never crop polaroids or instant photos – the chemicals in them will leak out and destroy the picture and your page). Trimming or cropping will also enable you to fit more images onto your layout.

When planning how to crop your image, decide what is the most important part of the picture. This is the section that you must keep; anything else can be cropped away. However, before you start, double check that you are not inadvertently cropping away any important elements or details.

must know

When cropping photos into specific shapes you can either use stencils or template shape cutters to help you, or you can work freehand. If you wish to mark your photo, place it upside down on a lightbox (so you can see the image through the back of the photo), then mark it with a graphite pencil or use a special photo pencil (see page 72).

Creating backgrounds

Cropped photographs can be used either singly or
layered to create delightful themed backgrounds or
landscapes. This usually works best when images are
chosen that contain colour schemes or themes that
are relevant to your particular project.

When cropping photos to use as background
decoration, try cutting photos to an appropriate
design, such as cropping garden pictures into tree or
flower shapes, or building water images from big
drops or splash shapes (see page 87).

Instead of simply cutting the individual pieces, you
can tear the edges (see pages 138-9). For extra
impact, use a mixture of both finishes.

Shapes and silhouettes

Silhouettes (or cutouts) are a useful scrapbooking
device that consists of carefully cutting around an
element in the photo (usually the subject) to partially
or completely remove the background, creating
a profile or outline of the image (see pages 78-9,
88-9 and 182-3).

Pictures can be cropped into different shapes and
sizes, and placed onto mats of a similar style (see
pages 138-9). Equally, your image can be cropped
into one shape (such as a circle) and placed on a mat
of a different type (a square, for example).

As with background images, you can also select a
shape for your main photos that is in keeping with
your subject matter, such as cropping your pictures
into strawberry shapes for a 'Fruit picking' layout.
Avoid using too many different shapes in one layout,
though. If in doubt, stick to one shape and recreate
that shape in a variety of sizes.

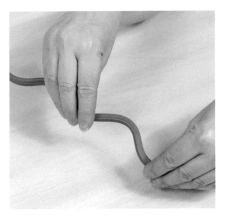

1 Flexible stencils are a simple, clever device for making patterned edges. Simply bend your stencil into the required shape; if treated with care, it will hold its position until you change it.

2 Use the stencil in exactly the same way as you would a fixed template, holding it firmly in place as you draw the pattern onto your photo or paper.

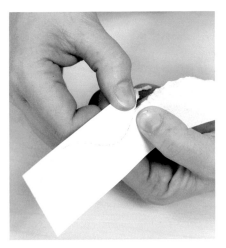

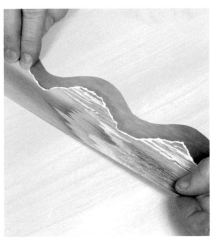

3 Tear your shape slowly, using the pencil line as a guide and keeping both hands as close to the marker as possible to give yourself maximum control of the tear.

4 Once you have cut and/or torn all your pieces into shape you can start playing with the arrangement: try using removable white adhesive tack to hold them in place.

Layering and merging

Pieces of photos from different sources can be interleaved together or mixed with other materials (such as paper, vellum or fabric) to create entirely new images. Alternatively, they can be used to make original backgrounds, frames and even page borders.

must know

Invisible glue and waxy-finish photo pencils are a useful addition to any scrapbooker's toolkit. Invisible glue allows you to fix vellums, acetates or superfine papers without any adhesive showing through to spoil the effect. Photo pencils can be used to mark the front surface of your image, then wiped away by placing the photo on a piece of scrap or waste paper and wiping pencil marks off with some tissue or kitchen paper. Again, all these items are available from a stationery or craft shop, or on the internet (see pages 187–8).

Enhancing your skills

Being able to combine or merge materials together will certainly give your designs an impressive look. Slicing up photos, particularly into little pieces, may feel an odd thing to do when you first start out. This is another good time to pull out those unwanted photos and do some confidence building. Improving your cropping skills will work wonders in terms of enhancing the quality of your scrapbooking pages.

Creating landscapes

Fresh and original backgrounds and landscapes can be created simply and easily with a few creative cuts and tears and a thoughtful selection of colours, shades and textures. In the example shown opposite, the seascape was created by layering a mixture of photographs of water and blue and white papers in various shades, weights, textures and consistencies. Contrasting visual textures have been created by using different methods to cut the photos of water. The torn edge of the photo near the top of the layout gives the effect of foam on the crest of a wave, while the neatly cut flowing edge of the water photo further down the layout suggests calmer waves. The edges have been cut and torn freehand, or by using a flexible stencil and a decorative-scissor pattern.

Photographs, paper, card, vellum and acetate have been
layered together to create this 'sea' background. The edges
have been cut in a variety of ways to represent the waves
and suggest a feeling of movement.

Merging slices

This technique can be used to merge two or more
photographs, or to create a background or mat from
either a mixture of images and paper or different
paper types or colours. An example is shown
opposite. To achieve this, take two equal-sized
pieces of coloured card, photos or, as here, one
photo and one piece of coloured card, and cut them
into equal slices. Arrange the slices on your page,
alternating between the two versions.

In the case of photographs, merging can work
particularly well with images that are the same or similar
in tone, as they will blend together and create a very
pleasing effect. Merging two different photos of the same
subject taken at approximately the same distance can
result in a compound image that looks like a panoramic
view. You can even cheat and slice through the different

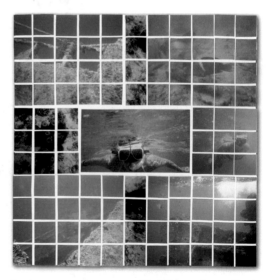

Turn the photo upside down and
mark straight, evenly-spaced
strips with a light pencil.

Create an unusual seascape with different photos sliced up
or (as here), cut into mosaic sections and merged together
around the main image.

photos, but mount them in their original order, pulled apart, with an equal space between each slice, so that the two (or more) photos are placed on the page side by side. When it works well, this effect will create the impression of being one single panoramic view.

Inspired variations

When cropping photographs, there are no limits as to how you cut them. Slices, segments and pieces can be symmetrical or asymmetrical, even or uneven, vertical or horizontal, diagonal, angled, straight cut, pattern-edged, freehand or torn. Just see where your inspiration takes you.

Move the slices around the page and do not stick them down until you are completely happy with your arrangement.

Go wild and experiment

Merge pictures of pets or wild animals with family portraits for a fun, if irreverent, effect; for instance, adding animal heads to human bodies (see opposite). Or do the reverse and place human heads on animal bodies instead. Alternatively, keep the different silhouettes intact, but alter the scale and compose a design in which small animals, flowers and insects appear as giants next to tiny people (see pages 78-9).

Improving the effect

When merging photos together, the layered edges can look a little untidy, regardless of how carefully you have cut out the different bits. To soften the edges and merge the cropped photos into a single layer, take a photograph of the finished picture, then print that out and mount it on the page.

1 Use a craft knife to carefully crop around any small details that are simply too difficult to reach with scissors.

2 Choose an adhesive that is suitable for use on small pieces, such as small-sized double-sided tape (usually available in its own dispenser).

3 This gorgeous colour scheme was chosen to reflect the warmth and rich earthy colours of the animal kingdom rather than the urban setting of the wedding.

Reducing and enlarging

Reducing and enlarging your photos, either with the help of your computer software or at your local copy shop, means that you needn't worry if your original photos are not quite the right size for your purpose. It also gives you scope for creating endless numbers of inventive and exciting scrapbooking designs.

Scale and proportions

Playing with scale or altering the proportions of people and objects is a great way to create layouts that are both imaginative and fun, as the example shown on these pages illustrates.

Once you have roughly planned your project, keep moving the different elements around your page or spread until you are happy with the arrangement. Once you have finalized your design, you can then either draw a quick sketch to act as a map and remind yourself where everything will need to go once you start actually sticking things down or, if you have a digital camera, take a snapshot of it instead.

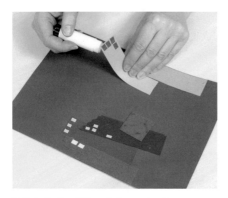

1 Only fix the different elements of your design to your page permanently once you are fully satisfied with the way your layout looks.

2 Begin with the background and work forwards, gradually building each layer in turn, double checking the positioning as you work.

Simplicity proved the key to success in this design, in which one single enlarged photo of a baby works perfectly against the cartoon-style paper cutout of the New York skyline.

Sections and segments

There are simple and ingenious ways of drawing attention to particular sections of your photos using framing techniques. Cutting your images into slices or segments, on the other hand, offers you countless possibilities for creating lively and dramatic photo displays.

must know

As with regular photo trimming or cropping, don't forget that you can always vary the effect by cutting your photos with decorative scissors to create patterned edges or even tearing your shapes to add extra interest.

Making internal frames

Instead of framing an entire image, you can draw attention to a small section or detail of your photograph with an internal frame. These can either be cut from card and fixed onto your image with photo mounts, or they can be cut from within the photograph itself to create a 'negative' frame, in which the background card can be seen through the gap.

When making a card frame, measure the part of the photo that you wish to frame, draw the frame onto the reverse side of your card and cut it out using a craft knife. Before you cut, double-check your measurements to make sure they are correct, or even try a draft version first on a piece of scrap. Use photo mounts to stick your frame in position. Other options for this type of frame-making include using string, ribbon, thread or wire to create your frame. These can be fixed onto the front of the photo or threaded through holes punched into the photo and stuck to the back to hold them in place.

To make a negative frame, either position your photo face down on a lightbox and draw your frame onto the reverse of your photo or use a wax photo-pencil on the surface of your image. Carefully cut the marked-up frame section out of your photo using a craft knife, holding your photo firmly in place as you cut. It is best to practise first on an unwanted photo.

Keeping the offcuts

As well as cropping photos and discarding the cropped pieces, you can incorporate both the cropped image and the offcut pieces into your designs. Leaving the outside crop in place can give better focus to the central image than removing it. For a more lively look, try angling or displacing the image and offcut(s).

Cutting and slicing

Cropping your image or images into vertical, horizontal, angled or even random slices or pieces is a fun way to add impact to your page (see also pages 74–5). Pieces can be even, uneven or a mixture of the

A simple effect can be created by framing a detail within the photo and drawing focus to a specific section.

This layout uses the technique of cropping around the main image, slicing the offcut section into random pieces in order to create a dramatic background. An internal frame is used to highlight the image of the boy at the centre.

two. Once cropped, there are numerous ways in which the pieces can be reassembled. Before you start slicing up your photos, though, decide on the focal point of your picture and slice around it. If you do decide to cut up the main image, keep the different pieces together, as this will prevent the focus from getting lost on the page.

You can create stunning designs with just one photograph or use two or more and interleave them together. Using sliced images on your page is an excellent way of highlighting action or movement in your photos, and will bring a burst of energy to your page. To make your task easier, choose photos that are similar in tone, mood or colour scheme. Two or more photos of a similar landscape or event, taken at a variety of angles or at different distances, are perfect for this kind of project, as are identical views taken at different times of day or even at different times of the year. These types of photos will blend well together and interleave beautifully, with any 'close up' images that you include looking all the more striking when surrounded by segments showing longer shots. Photo slices can also be used to create unusual backgrounds to your page (see pages 74–5).

Simple mosaics

Photo mosaics (see opposite) are simple to achieve and look magnificent. As with sliced images, they can be made either with just one photo or several. You can cut your mosaic 'tiles' into identical sized pieces or use a range of sizes. Lay your mosaic in a simple grid system or arrange your pieces in circles or spirals. Make a whole mosaic or build a mosaic border to frame your photo or edge your page.

must know

When working with photographs that have been sliced or cut into segments, don't lose sight of the central image. For best effect and to give your page a focus, keep the pieces of the photo in order, even when the image itself has been sliced through or segmented.

1 To create a mosaic effect, draw out an even grid pattern of squares or rectangles on the reverse side of your photo and number each square, to avoid any confusion later on. This may prove particularly useful if you don't have a copy of the original to refer to.

2 Cut out the pieces neatly, one strip at a time. Turn the pieces over and reassemble. Once you are happy, fix the pieces in place, keeping them straight or angling them slightly. For a more random effect, rearrange them, but leave the pieces of the main image in order, even if you choose to alter its position in relation to the other pieces.

Shapes, letters and numbers

Cropping your photos into shapes, whether freehand or to a template, can really spice up your page. Use geometric or random patterns or cut your photos into themed shapes or into appropriate letters and numbers.

Here the photo has been cropped into an oval shape to complement the circular frame.

Shapes

Cropping your photos into circles, ovals, squares, rectangles, triangles and hexagons will add interest to your photos. An equally pleasing effect can be achieved by adding internal shaped frames to your photo to accentuate either the subject or bring out certain details (see pages 80-1).

When cropping photos you can use geometric shapes or create your own patterns and trim your

By cropping these images into diamond shapes, you can create even more intricate patterns with your layout, such as this star shape (see pages 112-13 for the finished layout).

photos to fit them. You can also slice up your shaped photos (see page 74), working from the central image or main focus and slicing either side. To develop your technique, make several copies of the same image and crop them in different ways, to create lots of varied shapes.

Punches (see page 18) are a fun and easy way of creating shapes, letters and numbers from your photos (see pages 102–5 for details on how to do this). Use larger punches to crop your main images and then use miniature versions of the same pattern to punch photo scraps or matching paper to make eye-catching borders (see 'Borders', below).

Corners

The corners of photographs or shaped crops can be rounded to give them a gentler look. Corner-rounder punches (see page 105) are the best way to do this and are available in a range of styles. Even if you are tempted by the pattern-cut or decorated corner-rounders, a plain corner cutting punch is an extremely useful tool to have, as it can be used to soften sharp corners of photos, photo slices and even to round off corners of paper shapes.

Borders

Photo scraps, trimmings and paper offcuts can all be used to create edges, photo corners and borders, as can shapes, numbers and letters or leftover images. Simple decoration to each corner or a repeated image or series of images can look captivating on your page. Again, the easiest way to do this is to use a simple punch to create your shapes. Even a single border of squares, positioned straight or angled

watch out!

Sometimes straight-cut edges can look a little harsh on certain pages. To create a gentler look and soften the effect of any photo or paper shape, trim the edges with decorative scissors.

must know

Repetitions are a useful device and look great on any page. Repeat the exact image; use a mixture of uncropped shots and silhouettes (full or partial, see page 88); use copies of the image that have been reduced or enlarged to different sizes; or imitate the outline elsewhere on your page by adding paper shapes, cut to the same design as the subject itself.

around your page, will create an impressive look. Try also using a series of tiny portrait cutouts or crops, layered together to create a border, maybe in silhouette or cropped into geometric shapes. Or cut up the miniature 'thumbnail'-size index that comes with your prints, or print tiny digital images and cut these out to place around your page as borders.

Numbers and letters

Use the theme of your project or photograph to choose appropriate letters and numbers – this could be the place, event, subject's name, activity, age or house number. Use cropped photos for whole words or just the first letter and either cut numbers or letters whole from your photos, or combine pictures, picture pieces or photo scraps to form larger-style letters.

Transferring or repeating shapes

Tracing is a simple way of transferring a pattern from one image and applying it in a different setting. This is a great way to make use of any interesting shapes you find in books, magazines or other photos.

If there is a photo in your project with a particularly distinctive shape, such as the toucan, shown right, repeat the shape in your design by tracing it and using it as a pattern for cropping other photos. Alternatively, use it to create paper shapes or shadows.

Shapes, letters and numbers can be added to your page as they are or mounted, either separately or as a group. Cut out any mats to match the outline of your pieces or place shapes on panels or individual 'tiles', such as squares or circles. Apply self-adhesive foam spacers to add depth to your design.

When cutting out more general shapes, in order to add variety flip your template over to alter the pattern slightly.

Mark out letters or numbers on the reverse of your photo or, when the position of the image is crucial, on the front using a photo pencil.

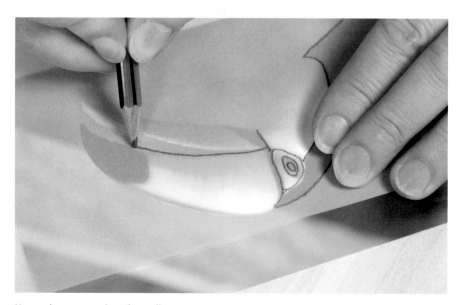

Use tracing paper and a soft pencil to copy your image, then place it face down on your paper and press firmly enough to transfer the lines.

Silhouettes

Using partial or whole silhouettes can add a touch of drama and originality to your page, drawing attention to your subject by bringing it into the foreground (see page 70).

In the case of partial silhouettes, only part of the background is removed. In some instances, certain details or features within the image can be silhouetted while the rest remains. You may want to silhouette the upper body of one of your subjects to give it focus or silhouette just legs, arms, hands or feet, or even your pet rabbit's ears – either to give it focus or to allow that part of the photo to overlap another image. In these instances, foam spacers can be placed behind the cutout detail, to offset it slightly and to bring that detail into the foreground.

A splash of colour

A particularly stylish technique to employ with silhouettes or partial silhouettes is to impose a colour detail onto a black-and-white version of the same photo, as illustrated in the project on these pages.

must know

To make a silhouette or partial silhouette you can either cut directly into the photo, or mark up your cutting path first with a waxy photo pencil (see page 72).

Plain yellow foam lettering balances the yellow of the taxi. The raised lettering highlights the 3D effect of the foam spacers, which add dimension and depth.

1 For this project you will need a colour and a black-and-white version of the same picture. Choose a picture that contains a strongly coloured image as its focus. Carefully cut out this image from your colour copy.

2 Apply foam spacers to either the back of your silhouette or the front of the identical image in the black-and-white version of the photograph. If the image is complex, apply the spacers to the silhouette itself, to ensure that adhesive will not be visible on the finished project.

3 Position your silhouette, ensuring that it lies perfectly on top of the equivalent image in the black and white photo.

Using digital photographs

Even if you have no intention of ever creating or designing any of your pages on your PC, having a computer, scanner and colour printer at your disposal can be a great asset.

Digital images

Having digital versions of your photographs available (either taken directly with a digital camera or scanned from regular photos) can be extremely useful. Even scrapbookers who prefer traditional methods and have no inclination to create computer-generated layouts or sophisticated photo manipulation techniques rely enormously on being able to scan and print photos at home.

Scanning

When scanning photos, depending on your software, you will have a choice of resolution settings – high resolution (around 300 dots per inch or dpi), medium (150 dpi), or low (72 dpi). For the best quality, choose

The quality of your photos will depend partly on the quality of your printer, but excellent results can be achieved even with very inexpensive models.

high-resolution images and save them in a TIFF file format. Many people save their photos as jpeg (or jpg) images, which are smaller files of a lesser quality, but these can produce good enough results (see page 163 for photo formats). However, the final quality will depend on the scanner, software and printer and the paper you use.

If you do not own a scanner, you can always have regular photos scanned and supplied back to you on CD at a photography store. Some stores even offer a do-it-yourself option.

Manipulating your photos

Having scans or digital images to work with means you can duplicate, reduce, enlarge or, for the more adventurous, make black-and-white or sepia tint versions of colour photos. Your software might also have an option to create special effects, such as sepia tone, embossing, charcoal and stained-glass. You may even be able to make repairs to photos that have been damaged or have deteriorated over time. When enlarging your photos always choose a high-resolution setting, in order to maintain the quality.

Storing photos

When storing digital images on your computer, make sure there is enough room on your hard disk, as pictures can take up a great deal of space. You can always transfer files to CDs to make more room, although if you do, it is best to make a back-up copy as well, just in case. If you have lots of photos, you might consider investing in an external hard drive which will give you plenty of space for your photos and other files and allow you to copy quickly backwards and forwards from your computer.

want to know more?

- **Choosing which photos to use 30-3**
- **Mounting your photos 48-9**
- **Making a kaleidoscope 144-5**
- **Silhouettes and shadows 98-9**
- **Cutting and tearing 102-5**
- **Weaving 110-11**
- **Photo montage 152-3**
- **Puzzles 118-21**
- **What is digital scrapbooking? 160-1**
- **Preparing your photos 162-3**

weblinks

- dpreview.com
- justamemory.com
- purplescraps.com
- scrapbook.com
- scrapjazz.com/topics
- ukscrappers.co.uk

4 Paper techniques

The endless array of gorgeous colours, textures, types, styles and finishes make paper an infinitely versatile and pleasurable medium to work with. There are papercrafting techniques that you can learn and effects that you can copy, but think of them as a starting point and a source of inspiration to encourage you to experiment for yourself and try out your own papercrafting ideas.

Paper folding

Cutting paper and creating paper shapes is an important part of creative scrapbooking. Adding paper folding and cutting to your scrapbooking palette will mean that you have even more decorative possibilities at your fingertips.

must know

Try folding and cutting a range of thicknesses of paper to experiment with different effects. The thicker the paper, the more difficult it will be to fold and the fewer folds and cuts you will be able to make. Wispy, thin paper will fold easily many times, allowing you to cut fine flowers with numerous petals, for example.

Snowflakes and flowers

One of the wonderful things about scrapbooking is that influences and ideas can flow in from any source. Paper folding is no different. Most of us can remember, as a child, the thrill of learning how to make chains of paper dolls or the art of folding and cutting paper circles to create snowflakes. These same techniques can now be put to fine decorative use in your scrapbook designs.

Accordion folds

To make chains of paper dolls or other shapes, fold your strip of paper, working it backwards and forwards into an accordion- or concertina-style fold (see page 96). Avoid making it so thick that you cannot cut through it easily – you can always make several shorter versions and glue them together.

Draw or trace your pattern onto the upper surface (star, circle, hand or even doll), taking the pattern right up to the edges on both sides so that the images join at the fold. Cut around your marked shape, taking care not to cut all the way through at the folds. Open out your chain and place on your page as a special decoration (see page 97) or stick the entire chain onto your page as a border, edging, or even a background to your title.

1 To make a paper flower (snowflake), take a square of paper, fold in half on the diagonal to make a triangle, then in half again several times.

2 Draw a petal shape (or other design) on one of the exposed faces, then, holding the paper firmly, cut around your pencilled guide.

3 Open out your finished flower, taking care not to tear any of the sections, and flatten to smooth out the folds. (See also pages 96–7).

Paper dolls

You can use a chain of paper dolls to add a sense of movement and perspective to your design, as in the layout shown opposite.

To make paper dolls, choose a strong image of a person with a clear outline for your central focus, like the photo of the man opposite. Make several copies of the image, cut carefully around each silhouette and paste them all together in a line to resemble a row of paper people. Repeating an image in this way will automatically give a feeling of movement to your layout.

To add an extra sensation of perspective, reduce or enlarge the copies of your selected photograph to different sizes, then crop and place them so that the images grow gradually larger across the page, giving the impression that the figure is travelling forwards towards you.

Finish off with a simple decoration – such as a raffia-tie 'jump rope' like the one in the layout opposite – to increase the feeling of movement in your design.

From boy to man...

This accordion-style picture book provides an extra special effect as it is a 'working' embellishment – the ribbon unties and it opens out to reveal a chain of baby pictures (see the layout opposite).

Adding extras with rubber stamps

Use rubber stamps to add extra visual interest to your folded-paper designs and colour them with paint, crayons, chalks or ink. In the layout shown opposite, the butterfly has been carefully positioned on the top right-hand corner of the journalling panel to give the illusion that it has just landed, having flown onto the design. The cheeky little sunflower placed in the bottom left-hand corner of the layout is designed to add balance to the page design. Naturally, these simple effects could be easily replicated with any number of different visual devices.

From boy to man...

What an adorable little baby Freddie used to be. Now look at him... He's still got the same smile, but where did he get that hat?

This project contains two types of 'paper chain' – the fold-out, accordion-style picture book and the paper-doll effect conveyed through the repeated images of the adult figure.

To make paper dolls like those in the project shown above, copy this template or create your own similar version.

Silhouettes and shadows

Silhouettes (whole or partial) can be used in your layouts in many different ways to create a variety of effects. Using your silhouetted image as a template to create paper 'shadows' of your original picture is just one such effect.

The semi-cutout couple look as if they could twirl off the edge of the page! (See pages 182-3.)

Mats and shadows

As previously mentioned, silhouettes (see pages 70, 88–9) can be used on their own, in layers, in groups, with other silhouettes or partial silhouettes and with uncropped photos. Cutting paper to the same shape and size as your silhouette gives you exact 'shadows' of your picture that can be used to add depth to your design. You can also crop a slightly larger version to make a contoured mat for your image. The matted silhouette can then be mounted on your layout as it is or placed back over the hole in your photo background (see right). Matting your photos in this way draws attention to the image itself.

Displacing your image

To add a little extra drama to your image, place a paper shadow cutout of your silhouette back on the picture, but 'displace' your actual image, placing it closer to the edge of the picture as if it is stepping out of the photograph. Alternatively, let it go walkabout and end up somewhere else on the page entirely!

You can also cut a silhouette from an enlargement of the original photo, then mat it as above and fix it, giant-like, to the smaller background. The greater the enlargement, the stronger the effect will be as your image bursts out of the edges of the frame.

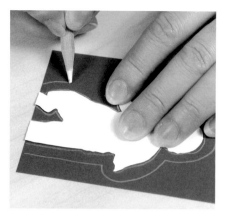

1 If your silhouette image appears in the middle of your photo, you may need an extra copy as the original version might be too damaged to use on your page.

2 Using your silhouette as a template, draw around it to create a guideline, then draw another outline slightly larger than the first to cut to create your matting.

3 Cut out your mat and glue down your silhouette, then stick the matted image back onto the photo, covering the position of the original image.

Using cutouts and layers

For the project shown opposite, the little girl's name –
Daisy – was the key source of inspiration for the theme,
while her pink t-shirt inspired the colour scheme. The
design demonstrates the use of built-up paper layers
and shapes and is constructed around a combination
of daisies of different types and styles, ranging from a
huge layered paper cutout to a silhouette made from
an enlarged photograph of a real flower.

Petal power

To enhance the design, make three or more folded
daisy heads as shown in the project opposite from
different shades and textures of paper using the
technique described on pages 94–5. These are to be
built up in layers into one flower, so decide upon the
order. Starting with the bottom layer, make each one
smaller than the last, so the petals of the lower layers
will be clearly visible. Add tiny punched flowers for
the middle of the daisy. Fix all the layers at the centre
only, leaving the petals to flutter.

The lettering and background are in identical
colours to the rest of the page. The alphabet buttons
and the bejewelled butterfly add texture to the page.

Punch flower shapes of varied
sizes and shades to use as
embellishments and to build
into the centre of the large
flower paper shape.

The big paper daisy may be the largest item on the page, but the pink-framed smiling photo on its pale pink foam mat is still the focal point.

Cutting and tearing

As with photos, paper can also be cut and torn to create a variety of different effects on your page. Shapes, mats, borders and backgrounds can be fashioned to suit the style of your design.

Using paper shapes for perspective

Simple but stunning effects can be created using only one shape. On the opposite page, a basic tree shape was cut in four different sizes from an assortment of papers. The tree shapes were then arranged on the page to give a feeling of perspective, with the larger foreground tree giving the impression of being much closer than the smaller one at the back (see also box left). Try out various compositions for yourself and watch your page shift and change as you alter the arrangement of the different shapes and colours.

Creating backgrounds

For the project shown on pages 104–5, a mixture of abstract tearing and sharp-edged cuts was used. Throughout the whole design straight, tidy lines are juxtaposed with random-shaped rips and tears.

The camouflage-style background of the layout was based upon the technique of 'pull-apart', in which a simple design is cut or torn and the various segments are simply separated and fixed to your page. This is a highly versatile technique which can be used in any number of situations, in order to create either backgrounds, mats, lettering or decoration. Either paper or a photograph can be used to create the effect, with the different pieces being torn apart from one another. Individual pieces are then laid back down in the correct order or sequence, with slight gaps left between the different pieces to allow the background to show through.

In this project (see the finished layout on pages 104-5), an adapted pull-apart style was used, with several of the segments replaced with other torn paper shapes to create an abstract overgrown forest feel. The dark brown paper has a wood-coloured core. When torn, the brown paper resembles pieces of tree bark.

Natural touches for texture

To add texture, beads were fixed to the right-hand page. Unstained, neutral-coloured wooden beads were chosen to give a natural tone. Liquid adhesive was spread across the bottom of the page and the beads sprinkled over this glue to create a forest floor.

On the left-hand page, an abstract pattern (see below) was pulled apart as described to form the background of the forest, with the torn shapes in

The clear-cut lines and clean colours of the tree shapes stand out beautifully against the solid black background.

The basis for the dense forest effect was a free-form hand-drawn abstract pattern that was then torn apart.

other earthy colours representing a raw wood and tree effect. The primary coloured 'paint' splashes were made using cutout paper templates (see page 57). The sightfinder in the top right-hand corner was created by simply cutting out a red circle then attaching it and adding two strips at right angles.

Sticky business

Different adhesives and techniques were used in order to attach the various items of this design. The self-adhesive alphabet stickers were matted on punch-cut square tiles before being positioned on the page. While a glue stick proved ideal for fixing the pull-apart torn paper shapes of the background, double-sided tape mounts were much more practical and neater for fixing the tiled vertical lettering, and

must know

No matter what techniques you are using, always allow your own personality to shine through. If an idea occurs to you that you find interesting, give it a go. Learning to scrapbook is about discovering what you like. One of the wonderful aspects of scrapbooking is that you can borrow and adapt techniques from any source and draw inspiration from every situation.

Use a square punch to make square mats on which to fix the alphabet letters.

mini glue dots were perfect for fixing the gun and sightfinder in position. The trees to the rear are held in place with double-sided photo mounts; foam-mounting squares were used to bring into relief the foreground tree. Liquid glue was used to fix the wooden beads of the forest floor (see below).

The two halves of this design are quite different in style, with the left-hand page busy with torn shapes in total contrast to the clean, clear lines of the right-hand page.

Using punches

Punches are easy to use and create immensely satisfying results. They can be used as photo cropping tools, to create paper shapes or to decorate borders and corners (see page 18).

Types of punches

Punches are available in all sorts of shapes, sizes and designs, including letters and numbers (see pages 187–8 for suppliers). Punch types include single shapes, multiple shapes, linear patterns, and corner rounders and shapers (in a choice of plain or decorative styles).

Smaller punches are excellent for making decorative shapes and for punching designs into mats or even into the photos themselves. Jumbo punches are ideal for cropping photos to particular shapes, as well as for making larger paper shapes

Place your punch on a flat, even surface, insert the paper and press down firmly to operate the punch.

Punched shapes can be used individually, built
up in groups or pieced together to create more
complex patterns and shapes.

1 Turn the punch upside down to check that your image is lined up correctly. Either operate the punch while holding it in both hands, or engage the cutter slightly to grip the paper, then carefully turn the punch upright and place it onto a hard surface to work it.

2 There are special punches that are designed for building decorative borders or shaping corners. To ensure that your border is even, measure the pattern itself, check the dimensions of the edges to be decorated and mark out a simple cutting guide on the reverse side of your paper.

3 For a more unusual effect, carefully punch half a shape out of the edge of your paper and then flip your half shape and line up with the negative cutout.

to be used as mats or for decoration. Punched shapes can be made from paper, light- or medium-weight card, photos or scraps.

Using punched shapes

Use your punch to decorate the edges of photos or, for a particularly inspired look, punch shapes into the edges of photos. Use the punched pieces as decoration, adding paper shapes to enhance the effect. This works extremely well with shapes that reflect something of the theme of your page, such as flowers or leaves for an outdoor scene.

Similar-themed punch shapes can work well together. For example, trees, leaves and flowers; dogs and cats; sun, moon and stars.

To add complexity, stack the same or similar shapes (such as flowers, squares or clouds) in different sizes together, using contrasting colours or a variety of shades to add to the effect. Or try creating your own punch art, by putting different shapes together to build a completely new image.

Punch shapes can also be placed in lines to make 'cheat' paperchains. This is great for shapes that are asymmetrical, such as leaves or hands, as alternate pieces can be flipped over to create a mirror-image.

Corner cropping

Corner rounders soften the effect of photos by cropping away tiny amounts of photo to create a smooth, curved effect (see page 85). Insert the corner into the punch at a diagonal, until it is firmly in place, then press. Punches are also available as decorative corner shapers to create a patterned edge or to punch shapes into your corner.

watch out!

If your punch is not making clean fresh cuts, check that there are no paper fragments stuck to the inside of the cutter. If there are, remove what you can by hand or with tweezers or give your punch a quick blast with a hairdryer set to 'cool'.

Weaving

Weaving is a good way to use up leftover paper and larger scraps. Weave backgrounds, mats for photos, titles or journalling, or simply use them as decoration. Use papers, photos or a mixture of the two.

watch out!

If choosing a tight weave, with no spaces between the strips, start by leaving a tiny gap between each strip. As you weave, your pattern will tighten; if you don't leave space to allow for this, your woven piece will tighten too much and will start to buckle.

Materials and finishes

Plain colours in different shades, contrasting colours or varied textures all work well together in woven designs. Weaving a solid colour with patterned paper or a photo will also give you lovely results.

Your weave can be loose – or open – with strips as far away from each other as you choose, or closed up tightly, as shown here. Strips of roughly 1cm (½in) in width give a nice finish and are manageable to work with, but it is entirely up to you what width you use.

For a more casual-style finish, leave out one or more strips from each piece and start weaving a short distance away from the edge. This will create a fringe effect with your woven pattern in the middle.

Finished weaves can be left as a square or rectangle or stuck onto a backing paper and cropped into a shape.

Photo weaving

To add a little texture to a single photo, simply weave two copies of the same picture together, or for a more unusual finish, use two versions, one printed in colour and one in black and white. This looks great as an embellishment or placed as a main image on your page. You can also experiment with weaving two different photos together.

1 Mark out your strips, making sure they are all the same size, onto the reverse side of each material, first deciding which is to be cut into vertical strips and which cut horizontally.

2 When using a photo, before you cut, number each piece. Lay your solid colour strips side by side, fixing them to the first (top) strip of the photo. Weave in remaining strips.

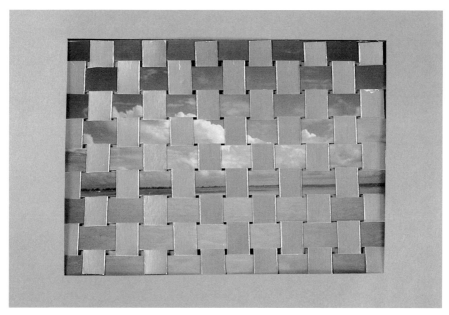

3 Finish off by securing the ends of the strips on the remaining three sides. Place your finished weave directly onto your background, or mount or frame it first.

Quilting

Photo quilts are remarkably easy to create and look wonderful. Use geometric shapes such as diamonds, squares, hexagons, triangles (made by cutting squares or diamonds in half) and fan shapes, or simply create your own design.

1 Trace your diamond shape onto the photos, isolating the parts of the images you want to use in your quilt design.

Laying out your quilt

Lay out the cropped photo pieces into a specific design or pattern or, once you have laid out an area of quilting, crop it into a different shape, such as a square or circle. Before you fix anything to your page, check the balance of the different photo crop pieces and ensure that there is a good mixture of lighter and darker tiles in your quilt. (See also pages 148–9.)

Trim the outside edges of the quilt with decorative scissors for a different effect or to draw attention to a particular area.

2 Crop the pieces, cutting just inside the lines to remove any marks, and arrange them into your photo quilt pattern.

3 Add a mixture of diamond and punched-out leaf shapes in autumnal colours to highlight the theme and colours of your project.

This project uses a number of different photos of the children for the central section, which is then framed by a more abstract surround of scrap cuts of seasonal trees. The delicate leaf shapes are loosely fixed to the page, using tiny dots of invisible glue.

Pop-ups

Pop-ups look complicated, but they are actually much easier to make than you might imagine. You just need to remember not to make the pop-up section too big to fit inside the folded pages or too heavy that it cannot stand upright and risks breaking away from the rest of the page.

must know

You may need to adjust the base of your pop-up slightly, depending on the thickness of your album. Thinner albums lie fairly flat and should not present a problem, but with thicker albums the pages may curve towards the centre fold, so you may need to increase the angle of the base and even shave away the base centre to prevent it from catching on the pages.

Photos, shapes and symmetry

Almost any picture or image shape can be used to create a pop-up, as long as the different elements are neither too long nor too big to fit within the folded pages. If you are concerned that this might be the case, do a trial run first using scrap paper (see page 116). It is not enough just to measure as, when the pages are closed, the folded items angle themselves towards the sides.

Layers

Pop-ups can be single or multiple layered, as shown here. However, it is best to use no more than four layers on any one page as the page will become too bulky to fold. Start by creating pop-ups of only one layer then experiment by gradually adding more.

Layers can be placed anywhere along the centre line. The only difference will be that the actual positioning will alter the length of your pop-up. The higher up the page you place the base, the shorter the pop-up will need to be, in order for it to fold away neatly. Therefore, if you want your pop-up to be taller, move the base further down the page so it can fold away. Layers do not need to be symmetrical, but the fold must line up with the centre of your page.

1 Mark out a template to make the base of your pop-up using card or sturdy paper. Add tabs at the bottom around 1.5–2cm (⅗–⅘in) in depth so you can attach the base to your page.

2 Cut out the base shape, fold in half, then fold the tabs towards the inward fold and apply adhesive. Strong double-sided tape is usually the most effective and least messy option.

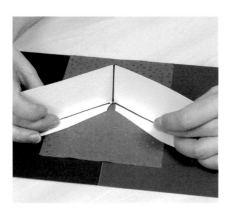

3 Arrange all the different elements on your page, to check the positioning. Make sure that your base is placed so that your pop-up will fit within the closed pages. When you are ready to start assembling, fix the pop-up base to your page, aligning the fold lines with the centre of your layout and angling it forwards slightly to point towards the front.

4 Close the pages and press down gently to make sure the base is fixed in place and check that it will open and close effectively. Gradually build up the rest of the pop-up and add in the remaining elements of your design.

When using more than one layer, place the bases slightly apart so that the images on the back layers are clearly visible.

Pop-ups can be used to display your photos or as a purely decorative device, with your photos arranged on the surrounding area. When attaching photos to the layers of your pop-up, make sure the background paper is robust enough to hold them without buckling or collapsing. If necessary, glue two pieces of paper together to add strength.

Album pages

The best place to put a pop-up project is towards the centre of your album. The reason for this is that when it is opened out at this point, there will then be an approximately equal number of pages either side, allowing your album pages to lie flat, and so giving your pop-up as stable a base as possible. If you are just including one pop-up in your album, such as the one here, then place it in the actual centre of the album to achieve the best effect.

The mirror-image fence was made from two copies of the same photo, one reversed, and used to decorate the base. The rocket firework was made by glueing together layer upon layer of punched stars, then applying star sequins.

Puzzles

Turning your photos into puzzles is a popular and charming scrapbooking technique. Choose between cutting your image into an actual puzzle or simply creating a puzzle effect by superimposing a puzzle-piece design onto your picture.

Creating a real puzzle

To crop your entire image into a working puzzle, firstly, follow step 1 (opposite) to make a jigsaw piece template. Next, mark up the back of your picture with a square grid, using the same dimensions as your puzzle template. Number each of the pieces in turn, to make reassembling your puzzle easier, then use your template to turn each square into a puzzle piece. Cut out, using small, sharp scissors or a craft knife, then reassemble using the numbers on the reverse for reference, where necessary.

Jigsaw pieces

The simplest puzzle shape to use is the symmetrical version shown here, as this requires only this one piece to make an entire puzzle or puzzle design. To fit the different pieces together and make your puzzle layout, simply turn the template by 90 degrees for each piece (see step 2, opposite).

There is no need to link your pieces into a jigsaw – you can arrange them individually on your page or simply use the puzzle piece as a template for cropping photo pieces or paper shapes as decoration. A good effect to try is to draw letters onto individual puzzle paper shapes and fit them together or place them side by side to form your page title.

1 Jigsaw templates are available, but you can easily create your own by drawing a square, then adding or cutting away small circles into each side.

2 Use your template and a photo-safe marker to draw a puzzle effect onto your picture in a grid formation, turning your template each time to lock the pieces together.

3 Cut away any incomplete pieces, then crop out selected edge pieces, using a craft knife, to create an unfinished, or 'work in progress', sort of look. This will also enhance the illusion of your photo being a real puzzle.

Little extras

The uncropped image on the left-hand page was mounted on the background using photo mounts. Three-dimensional pink flower stickers – designed to match the shade of the subject's cardigan – were then added as decorative corner mounts.

Shots of the city were scanned and reduced in size to create miniature images to use as embellishments. These were then mounted on mats that had been cropped using decorative scissors to make them resemble picture postage stamps.

Final touches were given to this page by adding an outline of the country made from red, white and blue strips of paper, to match the colours of the country's flag, and then cutting it out. This was then photographed on a white background with a

To create crumpled paper enhancements, crush your piece of paper into a ball – as tightly as you can – then carefully open it out and flatten it.

Holiday souvenirs make wonderful embellishments. If they are too cumbersome to go on your page, you can always photograph them and use the photo instead.

shadow behind it and printed onto glossy paper. The metal mesh mat was added to give texture and also because it is reminiscent of the ironwork of the Eiffel Tower itself.

The red and white ribbon adds extra texture and a final touch of fun and colour.

must know

When using three-dimensional items on scrapbooking pages, choose an album that allows you to place spacers between the different pages so that items don't get damaged. Placing pages in page protectors or plastic holders prevents your fragile items from being harmed and protects photos on the opposite pages from being spoiled.

Stained glass and mosaics

Mosaic style and stained-glass effects can be made with whole or partial pictures. They also provide a perfect opportunity for using up photo scraps or unwanted pictures.

must know

To create a different effect, mat each of the pieces in a contrasting colour or different shade and then place them on your background. This shattered glass effect can also be used for dramatic titling: simply slice up a title panel in the same way, mount each of the pieces and reassemble them on your page.

Paper impact

When you look at a finished scrapbooking mosaic it will probably be the photographic element that catches your eye. However, truly successful mosaics are entirely dependent upon the choice of background paper, as it is this paper 'cement' peeping through the gaps between the photo 'tiles' that holds the design together and shows the mosaic off to its best advantage. Don't forget that coloured papers can be used for mosaic tiles, too, or combined with photos to brighten your design.

Mosaic tiles can be laid out on a single-colour background or certain sections can be matted in different shades or colours to give focus to those areas and add visual impact to your project.

Patterns and layouts

Lay out mosaics into simple square grid patterns (see pages 82–3) or build them into more complex arrangements, using different-sized pieces and shapes, or even tearing the edges for a more unusual and less formal look.

As well as using mosaics to create entire pictures or scenes, use the same technique to create magnificent backgrounds for your photos or silhouettes. Mosaic technique can also be used to create frames and borders or to craft tiny mosaics to use as embellishments. A small square punch is ideal for punching photo and paper scraps for these purposes.

Using random shapes

Instead of cutting your photos into even slices or segments (see pages 74–5 and 81–3), for increased drama, cut your photographs into random shapes instead. You can then reposition them in the correct

Artistic cropping can eliminate any need for decorative extras on your page as this stunning random-cut, shattered-glass mosaic demonstrates.

order (see previous page) or place them in a more abstract arrangement. However, you need not limit yourself to using one photo: take pieces from as many as you choose in order to create your desired effect.

Stained-glass effects

A stained-glass look works well on the scrapbooking page. Crop your photo(s) into either large chunks or small pieces and place them on a black background, pulling the pieces of the photo apart from each other slightly to allow the black to show through. Pieces can be reassembled into the same arrangement as they appear in the original image, or repositioned, to alter the image. Stick down with glue dots.

Another further option is to cut up photo scraps into small, regular or random shapes or shards and use them to fill a design or shape of your choice – such as a tree, a large flower, a boat or building.

This country-style stained-glass effect is perfectly complemented by the titling tiles and house decoration in the same colour as the house itself.

Larger shapes, natural lines

Instead of simply cutting your photos into small pieces, crop your pictures into their different parts. Ideally, for this you will need images that are not overly busy and that contain clean lines and distinct areas which can be easily cropped into silhouettes.

You do not need to be too exacting for this purpose, but make sure that you cut neatly. Use small, sharp scissors to create a clean fluid line, however general it might be, around each area.

Once you have cut the picture into as many silhouettes as you require, take any number of these and break each one down further, following the natural lines that appear on the photo to separate them out into their component parts. Mount the finished pieces on a plain black background.

The project shown on the opposite page is a very basic example of this technique, made up, as it is, of chunky portions and rounded shapes that do not fit together very precisely. However, this adds to the somewhat 'country farmhouse' feel of the image.

Variations on a theme

A valuable exercise that will give you the opportunity to experiment with new techniques and can sometimes give you unexpected and wonderful results is to take a previous design or idea and give it a new twist. For example, the 'Taxi' project on pages 88–9 could be reworked to add a stained-glass effect. (Don't forget to add black mounts behind each letter of 'TAXI'!) In this instance, adding a crisp black background to a black-and-white image will give even more prominence to the yellow highlights.

want to know more?
- Using colour 42–3
- Adding texture 44–7
- Improving your designs 56–7
- Cropping 66–71
- Merging 72–7
- Reducing and enlarging 78–9
- Making fold outs 132–5
- Using paper tricks 154–7
- High days and holidays 174–7
- Celebrations 180–1

weblinks
- cannycrafts.com
- lakelandlimited.co.uk
- paperchase.co.uk
- papercraftsmag.com
- papercraftz.com
- tollitandharvey.co.uk

Cut out the component parts of your picture, making the pieces as large and general or as small and detailed as you like.

5 Moving on

As you become more experienced, you will begin to come up with new ideas and possibilities for your scrapbooking pages. Sometimes this may involve learning completely new skills and techniques, but often you will find that you can create wonderful new projects by simply taking a familiar technique a step further, altering it slightly or adding to it to create fresh and original designs.

Layering and building

Photo crops and paper shapes can be combined together to build entirely new landscapes as a background to your project. It does not really matter where the various photo pieces come from, but they will need to be appropriate in texture and colour.

Creating new vistas

Building scenes out of pieces of photos, photo scraps and paper cuts can be done in numerous ways. On page 131, wave-shaped pieces have been stacked horizontally to create a seascape. Diagonal or vertical slices or sections can also be used to build pictures, whether neatly cut or torn-edged (see pages 74–5).

Tile mosaics

Use square (or rectangular) punches to crop lots of squares out of paper and photo scraps, then use a

A stunning landscape photo made into a simple tile mosaic provides a great backdrop to your holiday snaps and ties in all the different elements of your layout.

corner rounder to soften the corners. Use these 'tiles' or 'bricks' to build a mosaic-style background (see pages 82-3).

Improving your designs

There is no need to constantly come up with new ideas – sometimes it is better just to work on improving your old ones. The design for the retirement project on pages 130-1 grew out of the layering exercise on pages 72-3. Here, more variation and dynamism has been added in the shaping of the waves, as well as including the dolphin detail, enhanced by giving it a three-dimensional effect. The upper background image was made by enlarging a sailing photo to fit the width of the page. The silhouetted figures are fixed to the boat with foam spacers.

Fine wooden beads are used in this collage-effect layout to represent the forest floor (see pages 104-5).

Creating collages

Collages are formed by taking a mixture of materials and building them into a picture. Scrapbooking draws heavily on collage techniques, whereby sandpaper, fragments of wood, fabric, paper clips, seeds and all sorts of memorabilia can be introduced. Instead of merely using items as decoration, try creating a picture, finding appropriate uses for the different items. Sandpaper could be used to represent a beach, for example, while a feather might be used as the basis for a bird shape, or paperclips to build a fence, or maybe buttons to represent the wheels of a car.

Using black and white

You can also create captivating results by mixing colour and black-and-white photos, perhaps blending black-and-white and colour copies of an identical image, like the Taxi project in Chapter 3, pages 88-9.

must know

Black-and-white photographs can look fantastic in a layout when set against a colour background, as the colour will enhance the quality of the photo and the black adds richness and depth to the colour itself. Equally, neutral tones (such as beige or natural wood colours), combined with single bright colours (such as sky blue), are a great match.

1 Use rub-down lettering to create wonderfully clear titles. Draw faint pencil guidelines onto your page to keep your wording straight or use a ruler to guide you.

2 Mount the blue title panel onto a pattern-cropped textured white paper panel in order to make it stand out clearly from the blue sky colour of the background.

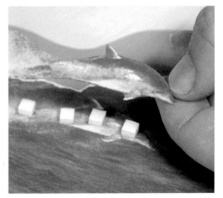

3 Mount a selection of cut and torn-edged papers and photos cropped into wave shapes, layering together to build them into an impressive seascape (see pages 72–3). Here, a dolphin detail in one of the photos has been deliberately selected and arranged so that it is visible through the next layer of 'waves'.

4 Silhouette an enlarged copy of the same dolphin photo and use foam spacers to fix it over the top of the background dolphin image, adding depth to the page and making the dolphin look as if it is jumping out of the water.

Anchors away
for a
Happy
Retirement

The sea is the most impressive feature of this layout. The three-dimensional effect of the dolphin jumping out of the water is achieved with foam spacers, and the same effect has been applied to the men at the top of the layout.

Making fold-outs

To add an element of style and surprise to your layout, turn your scrapbooking page into a fold-out by adding side flaps that close like doors (see the sample design overleaf). A fold-out design would also be perfect as a freestanding project to give as a gift.

must know

'Shaker boxes' (see the sequence opposite) can be used to brighten up any design. They are box-like embellishments that are added to a page as a simple decoration, filled with glitter, beads or sequins (page 134), or used to display your main image (see pages 174–5).

Creating your fold-out page

In order to create a fold-out project (see the finished example on pages 134–5), the folding background should be twice the width of your actual page. If you have a large enough piece of coloured paper, you can cut the entire background from one sheet, then measure it into four horizontal bars, folding the two outside sections inwards to create the door flaps. The centre section will then be fixed to your scrapbooking page.

If your sheet of coloured background paper is not large enough to use for the side panels as well, then cut them separately from a different piece of paper, allowing an extra 4cm (1½in) in width to act as tabs for glueing the flaps in place. Next, cut a centre panel and fix it over the top. In the sample project featured on pages 134–5, a patterned paper was chosen to enhance the design.

Setting the scene

The sample layout shown (see overleaf) creates an atmosphere, rather than building a detailed picture background. However, the pretty colour scheme, the opening-door effect, the mirror, the 'dressing up' montage silhouette on the right-hand flap and the spotted central background panel that looks like trendy wallpaper all suggest a young girl's bedroom without actually showing any of it in detail.

1 To make a shaker box, cut a shape (e.g. a flower) for the base and make a larger version for the lid.

2 Stick foam spacers (either squares or strips) around the edge of the box base.

3 Draw a central outline to create the window in the lid of your shaker box.

4 Score a cross shape in the middle then use small scissors to snip away the central panel. Cut a piece of acetate and stick it to the back of the lid, over the hole in the central panel. (You can buy sheets of acetate from good craft or stationery shops.)

5 Use tweezers to remove the backing on the adhesive foam spacers. Fill this area with glitter, then press the lid onto the foam to seal.

Extra embellishments

You can add extras to your fold-out design like those shown here. The shaker box in the bottom left-hand corner of the central panel is a rather subtle touch, but extremely effective, adding a little extra colour and sparkle to the piece. The ready-made built-up stickers that are used both inside the layout and as decoration on the outside of the 'doors' add an extra touch of sophistication, while the cartoon crown on the central image draws attention to the girl.

Taking its cue from an advent calender, each of the rectangular panels in this project is a little door that opens up to reveal a surprise. The small panels contain more pictures while the large title panel is filled with journalling.

Moving parts

The addition of moving parts makes this fold-out layout more interactive. For example, the small, montage silhouette on the right-hand flap of the featured project can be moved slightly. In this case, the different pieces were cut out, mounted on card and then held in place with tiny brads – one at the shoulder, to fix the arm and allow the hand to move up and down, and one at the base of the neck allowing the head to 'nod' when touched.

Secure a ribbon around the page to keep the 'doors' closed. Hold in place with heart-shaped paper clips.

SUPER COOL SIS

Journalling

Aside from your photographs, journalling can be considered to be the most important element of your scrapbooking page, as it is through your journalling that you can share information about the photos as well as telling your own story.

Thinking it through

Good planning is the key to successful journalling. Your text may be the last element to be added to your page, but when designing your layout – and long before you stick anything down – you need to think carefully through the positioning, style and format of both your journalling and any titling and captions. Sometimes when you are starting out in scrapbooking, it can be easy to become absorbed in the design and decoration of the purely visual elements only to discover at the end that there is no room left on the page for your journalling. Don't let this happen to you!

Positioning and wording

Text and captions can be positioned next to individual photos or placed separately in its own special area. It can run horizontally or vertically, angled or straight, or even be shaped to fit a particular pattern (see pages 50–1, 60–3).

Try to write in the way that you would speak, keeping your journalling as informal as possible. Don't be fooled into trying to create unnecessarily flowery language – it is your voice we want to hear. Practise speaking your text out loud first, or even recording it and playing it back to yourself.

Jessica's rabbit

...but I don't want to come indoors yet...

......can I bring Roger in with me?

......just this once, PLEASE? He really misses me.

...guess I'll just stay in here with him instead. Goodnight!

This simple sequence works to support the series of photos, giving a sense of Jessica's character and making her thoughts and feelings abundantly clear.

Here, this journalling takes the form of cherished words for the child when she's older.

Creating timelines

Another possibility in scrapbooking is to create a timeline or a feeling of time passing. This can be an encapsulation of a person's whole life or a description of an incident or event that lasted only a few minutes.

must know

Creating scrapbooking pages is a form of storytelling, so make sure that your page does just that. Choose a story that will capture the audience and set a particular mood. Make sure your story has one or more lead characters whose tale is allowed to unfold. And finally, make sure that your story has a beginning, a middle and an end.

Choosing your words

This project shows that you can communicate very clear information using a minimum of words. All that is required is sufficient detail to get across the information needed to give your page a context of some sort and to make the story within it abundantly clear. Your words need to complement your photos, making your page even more charming.

The idea of a timeline is visually reinforced by using an actual 'line' to hang the photos from. The tags hung at different angles look as if they are blowing in the wind.

Details that you might want to include are: 'Who are the people in the photo?'; 'Where and when is it taking place?'; and 'What exactly is going on?'. You can also describe the thoughts and feelings of those involved (see page 137), or even include your own. If you like, add a piece of poetry, a quotation, proverb or saying that resonates with your theme.

Using vellum

The transparency of vellum makes it ideal for journalling, as it is subtle enough to blend in to your background but also creates a rather lovely layered effect (see also pages 72–3). Writing your wording onto separate vellum panels first allows you more margin for error than lettering directly onto your page would give you.

These photos were cropped to create a torn-edge effect, adding an informal and natural tone to the piece.

2.42pm

2.50pm
back safe
& sound

Project ideas

Although photographs can be a great source of inspiration for new projects, sometimes it can be helpful to look elsewhere for information and ideas. Keep an open mind and experiment.

watch out!

Don't be afraid to borrow ideas from any source, but if you do decide to use a scrapbooking idea that you have taken from someone else's work, don't get caught in the trap of simply copying their work. Even if you like their style, let your imagination loose and see what possibilities your own creative flair can come up with.

Outside sources

Books, magazines, catalogues and even newspapers can be a wonderful source of new and fresh ideas for scrapbooking projects. Museums and galleries of all sorts are full of thought-provoking possibilities and are always excellent places to visit, particularly if your creativity is flagging and you are in need of a boost.

Sometimes, nature can provide the most charming and imaginative of ideas. If you are stuck for a project theme, try taking a walk in the countryside; you will be amazed what comes to mind when your lungs are full of fresh air and you are surrounded by natural beauty.

Internet options

Don't forget that out in cyberspace there is a huge scrapbooking world just waiting to be discovered. You can find endless amounts of information on any subject. Use your internet search engine (such as Google or Yahoo) to find an array of information and images. You can also visit various scrapbooking or craft sites that will enable you to see the work of other people, get answers to any questions you may have or give you hints and tips on all aspects of scrapbooking and other related areas of interest. To get started, have a look at some of the suggested websites on pages 186–8.

Hats off for baby boo

A word of advice... it's no good letting your parents choose your hats. I did it once and look at how my Dad dressed me. I was mortified. What exactly is that thing on my head supposed to be? A horse? A short-necked giraffe. He looks happy enough, sure, but that was the end as far as I was concerned. After that I put my foot down. Nope, from now on, it's me that makes the the the decisions in the hat department.

Practically any subject can be used as the basis for creating fun and imaginative scrapbooking projects.

A few possibilities

Here are just a few ideas for possible project titles:

Spring showers	Dancing days
Summer days	Fitness fanatic
Winter wonderland	Bathtime bubbles
Roses are red	Glittery girl
Angel face	Baby new shoes
Little boxes	Musical mayhem
Lazy days	Naughty little brother
Walking the dog	Sand, sea and sunshine
Look who's smiling	Ladybird, ladybird
Best friends	Keeping secrets

want to know more?

- Sections and segments 80-3
- Shapes, letters and numbers 84-5
- Designing a basic layout 36-41
- Using colour 42-3
- Adding texture 44-7
- Choosing lettering 50-1
- Improving your designs 56-9
- Layering 70-1
- Creating action 146-7
- Occasions to remember 182-3

weblinks

- momscorner4kids.com/fonts
- scrapbook.com
- stampin.com/tips.htm
- thequotegarden.com
- twopeasinabucket.com

6 Special effects

Kaleidoscopes, optical illusions, montages
and all sorts of paper tricks are, in essence,
invaluable techniques that can be as
straightforward or as complex as you choose
them to be. Combining and applying simple
techniques with a little creative flair and
imagination will almost certainly result
in utterly breathtaking designs.

Making a kaleidoscope

Kaleidoscopes are a fun way of using repeated images to create interesting, dynamic patterns. Choose photographs with strong images or repeated patterns and good clear colours.

Basic kaleidoscopes

Kaleidoscope patterns may look complicated but they are remarkably easy to make, if you choose the right image or images. You can create a kaleidoscope with as few as four photos (two copies of the original versions plus two reversed copies – flip them to get a mirror image in your photo manipulation software).

Photo kaleidoscopes can be used to frame a central image (either matted or left plain), as shown here, or used to fill the entire area. If you are using them as a border or frame, you can either use a larger version of the photo for your central image or maybe a different photo entirely.

Assembling your kaleidoscope

Place your photos roughly how you wish to use them, alternating the original and the reversed photos so that they mirror each other. Decide upon the amount of overlap you need at each corner and crop your photos according to the method described in the caption, left.

Assemble the pieces on your chosen background, making sure that the cut edges line up correctly, then fix into place, adding the central image – if there is one – last. If you are not using a central image, don't worry if you are left with an empty space at the centre point of your kaleidoscope. You

To mitre corners neatly, place one corner photo on top of the other, and tape together the overlapping corners on the reverse, making sure the patterns or images line up. Turn the photos over and, using a ruler, mark a cutting line on the reverse of the photos at the intersection. Cut through the two layers with a craft knife.

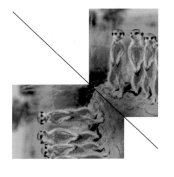

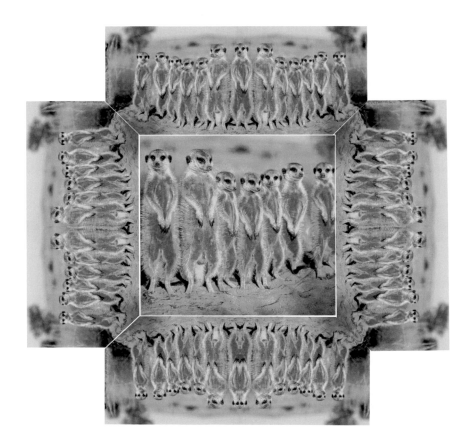

can either leave it and simply allow the background colour to show through, crop it into a shape of its own or fill it with another mini kaleidoscope made with scraps from the original photo(s), another photo, a paper shape, a sticker or an embellishment.

Advancing your technique

Experiment with using different numbers of photographs in your kaleidoscope – anything from four to 16 is quite usual, although it is easiest to start with eight, or even four, for your first attempts.

Creating action

Imbuing your layout with a sense of movement and action can be easy to achieve and very effective. Including bright, bold colours immediately adds a feeling of energy and activity, while using angled pieces instead of straight lines creates a sense of motion.

must know

Even in a busy layout such as that featured, make sure that your design is balanced. The colours and various angles may at first give the design a slightly random feel, but, in fact, it is symmetrical in form. In the layout opposite, the cannon and cannonballs mirror and balance the positioning of the title and the tiny framed picture.

Angles, colours and unity

For a layout full of movement like the one illustrated opposite, use layers of coloured card and paper cut at acute angles and laid over one another to maximize the impact of the colours and the different shapes. In the layout shown, the white outline shape of the circus tent was fixed onto a primary blue background. It was then adorned with shaped strips of bright red card or fabric to create the striped effect of the 'big top' tent. Use fabric or card scraps to make further embellishments, such as the cannon and cannonballs shown opposite and the flag on the big top.

Position key elements at an angle, such as the central silhouetted figure shown, to imply explosive movement. Use a lively contrasting colour, such as yellow or orange, to mount your title panel, then frame your contrasting image – in this case the 'city' picture – in a pretty, textured surround. The combination of bright colours with the extreme angling and overlaying of the many and varied shapes is what makes this design so vibrant.

Final details and extra texture

In the sample layout shown, dramatic final touches include a fuse using wire-threaded beads and a multi-layered explosion to add texture, made out of paper offcuts, star punches and shiny star sequins.

OFF TO WORK...
life's a circus

The combination of bright colours, different textures and
layered items in this design creates a powerful sense of
movement and action which makes it leap off the page.

3D illusions

This fabulous building block effect is actually made by cropping photos using a single diamond shape. Combine three diamond-cropped photos to create one or several individual cubes, or alternatively stack blocks together into a tower.

Isolating your image

Choose your photos carefully to make sure that they fit within the 'diamond' format: you may need to enlarge or reduce some of them. Remember, all your images need to be the same way up.

Building your blocks

Construct your blocks leaving an even space around each cube face to allow the background to show through, thus defining the individual images. Use photos for each of the planes or make some in coloured paper in a contrasting colour to the background. Also, add decorations or lettering (see opposite). The puppy photo album is affixed with a brad, a small paper fastener with a head and two prongs which are pushed through the paper and bent outwards to prevent the brad from being able to come back out.

1 Mark out blocks onto your background paper with a block template, or by building your design using a single diamond shape to guide you. Use the same template to mark your photos with a special wax-finish pencil (see page 72).

2 Place your photos (and other decorations) on the 'block' mat. When you are happy with the design, stick everything down, first rubbing out any pencil guides that might still show around the edges of your images.

A 'name tag' style and informal lettering
were chosen for the titling of this page, while
a miniature photo album of puppy pictures
was fixed to the page with a brad (see left).

Simple optical illusions

Creatively cropping and layering your images to play photographic tricks and create bizarre illusions within your layouts is an irresistible technique that is entertaining and easy to effect, and can produce remarkable results.

must know

Using speech-bubble captions is a delightful way to add journalling to your page. Cut your own shapes, either freehand or to a template, or search and download patterns from the internet (see page 187). You can even buy packs of speech-bubble stickers from craft shops or on the internet, some of which are blank for you to fill in with your own lettering or ready-printed with wording.

Combining techniques

The creation of simple optical illusions with your photos relies upon the combination of several different techniques which are covered elsewhere in this book. In the sample layout shown opposite, the background image has been double-matted to provide depth and perspective (see page 48). The silhouetted figures have been set at an angle to suggest movement (see page 146), and also mounted on foam spacers to enhance the sense of them floating above and through the scene (see page 130). The speech-bubble title and cartoon-style London bus have also been mounted on foam spacers; these make them cast shadows, which cause them to stand out even more sharply and develop the sense of the background receding.

For a smoother finish and a more merged effect, photograph your own finished photo montage before mounting it on your page (see page 76).

Selecting suitable photographs

Practically any photograph is suitable for layering to craft imaginary worlds or cropping to create illusory tricks. What will make your task a great deal easier, though, and give you more flexibility, is if you have the facility to reduce and enlarge your own photos.

In this layout, the caption cleverly doubles as a title to the page, due to its prominence and position on the page. The caption, silhouetted figures and bus sticker are mounted on foam spacers, making the background appear even more distant.

Photo montage

Photo montage can be as simple or as intricate and detailed as you wish. Photo pieces and cutouts can be reassembled to create a new shape, used to create backgrounds and borders, or even used to decorate large letters and numbers.

must know

Gels (see page 53) are unusual decorative items which are available in a range of styles, colours, shapes and sizes, and are sold by most craft suppliers. Lighter colours and larger shapes may need to be fixed to the page using invisible adhesive.

Simple montage

A delightfully simple montage effect can be created by assembling silhouettes of cropped photographs on unusual mats or borders and mixing them with bold, colourful paper cutouts, as shown in the layout below. Choose an overall background that will allow your cutouts to stand out clearly on your page, if necessary mounting your photos on mats in tones or

colours that will ensure that they are as prominent as possible. Here, the rich green background is reminiscent of the baize of a traditional card table, while the white photo mounts, cut to resemble playing cards, show off the photo cutouts perfectly.

Leaving one photo in your design uncropped will give it a different visual impact. In this layout the eye is drawn to the central uncropped 'Dad' photo, while the colourful corner mounts, made from red and green card scraps, make this image stand out even more.

Use punches (see page 18), pre-purchased stencils (see page 17) or your own freehand design to make decorations to enhance your layout. Here the simple, bold shapes of the four different playing card suits cut out in two different sizes make a strong statement, while using textured card enhances their effect.

The double corner mounts are made by punching different-sized squares in contrasting colours and then sticking them together with mounting tape.

Using paper tricks

This clever design (see the finished layout on page 156) looks good enough to eat and provides a fun and unusual way of presenting several pictures in one project.

watch out!
If you decide to give patterned edging to your 'cake', either use decorative scissors to start with or trim it with patterned scissors before you slice up the segments.

Improving your techniques

This particular project is fairly complex and incorporates several similar techniques that we have covered so far. It involves creating a paper cake top in equally divided segments, each of which can be lifted up to reveal a photograph beneath. The 'My sweet sister' project on pages 134–5 employs this advent calendar-style effect in a simpler manner. Have a go at one or two more straightforward projects first – like the 'My sweet sister' design – before tackling this one. Practising with projects that have been covered earlier on in the book will give you a chance to brush up your paper manipulating skills and will also prevent you from wasting precious 'good' paper unnecessarily on more challenging projects like this one.

Precision

Marking up the cake segments evenly and making sure the folds are crisp and neat is vital to the final look of this project. Equally as vital is making sure that each of the folds is glued evenly into place in the correct position. If not, your finished piece will look messy.

Try out the different techniques described here as many times as you need until you feel truly confident in your abilities and happy with the end

1 Use round templates (or household items) to make three circles in total: two smaller in size – one in white (or scrap paper) and the other in pink, and a larger one in blue.

2 Fold the white circle in half, then into thirds, then open it out and mark each fold. Use the template to transfer these marks and the centre point of the circle onto the pink paper.

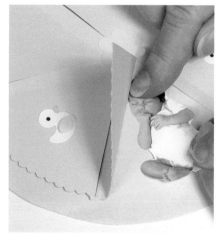

3 Draw a small circle at the centre of your pink paper, then, using the marks taken from the template, draw solid lines up to the centre circle, dividing your paper cake top into six segments. These are cutting lines. Next, add parallel dotted lines (for the folds), a few millimetres away from each of the solid lines.

4 Cut along the solid lines (but only cut up to the edge of the centre circle). Carefully fold back each segment along the dotted line, creating a tab for each segment. Apply glue to each and stick the pink cake top onto the blue base. To finish, fix photos of the babies under each segment flap.

The finished scrapbook page, fashioned in an advent card type design, which cleverly hides earlier pictures of the twins' lives.

Under each piece of cake is a different photograph. This kind of format is also ideal for sequences of photos of a particular event, or a selection of pictures placed in chronological order.

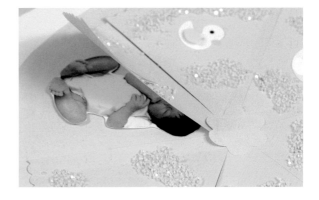

results. The key is never to rush: just work steadily and carefully on each step in turn.

Selecting your paper

You will need to choose your paper carefully for this project, particularly the paper you are planning on using for the cake top, because if you choose a type that is too heavy it will be awkward to fold neatly, as this top section of the design is actually fairly small. Equally, you don't want to select a paper that is too thin either, because even though that might make it much easier to work with, the result will be that your cake segments are flexible and the finished cake top will be fragile.

Templates

When it comes to simple geometric shapes like squares and circles, you don't necessarily need tailor-made templates. Often items that you can find around the house are ideal for this purpose; cups, saucers, plates, tins, tops, lids – even old CDs – can be used for drawing around to create circles of different sizes. For this project you need two circles with a difference in diameter of around 2cm (roughly 1in). Depending on the size of your page, a bowl, plate or saucer should be perfect.

The icing on the cake...

This pretty layout lends itself to a little extra decoration to really brighten it up and make it something special. The blue and pink baby clothes stickers provide just the right touch, while the baby toy and duck stickers make perfect cake decorations. The coarse, sugary-looking, pastel-coloured glitter is perfect as frosting to decorate the top of the cake.

want to know more?
- Accessories 52–5
- Merging 72–7
- Reducing and enlarging 78–9
- Using punches 106–9
- Weaving 110–11
- Quilting 112–13
- Pop-ups 114–17
- Stained glass and mosaics 122–5
- Layering and building 128–31
- Celebrations 180–1

weblinks
- creativexpress.com
- scrapbookers playground.com
- stencil-library.com
- tollitandharvey.co.uk

7 Digital scrapbooking

Just like traditional scrapbooking, digital scrapbooking (also known as electronic or computer scrapbooking or even sometimes 'digi scrapping') is a means of storing and preserving your photos and memorabilia in creative and interesting ways, but using digital technology instead of paper and scissors. However, even the most die-hard traditional scrapbookers often adopt a digital approach to a certain degree, relying on digital cameras to take photographs and using computers, scanners and printers to reproduce images and create text and lettering.

What is digital scrapbooking?

If you take photos using a digital camera, print photos, generate text from your computer or use the internet to order supplies online or do some scrap research, you have already entered the wonderful world of digital scrapbooking.

Going digital

At first, it may take time getting to grips with your chosen software program, particularly if it is one of the more complex examples such as Adobe Photoshop. However, the upside is that eventually you will have even more control over your designs than you would with paper layouts. You can crop, resize and edit your photos simply and easily; use digital elements again and again, altering the colour to match your layout (see below); or even create and manipulate your own decorative items, either by photographing such items as bows, hinges, flowers or tags, or producing your own elements graphically using your computer software. You will always be able to delete or undo any

Digital scrapbooking is extremely cost effective, as you can reuse items, adjusting them digitally to suit your layout. Print out items and use them in your regular scrapbooking pages, as well.

steps that you are not happy with, or change your mind and move things around (but always keep a back-up copy, just in case). In addition, your workspace needs only to be large enough to hold your computer and peripherals (printer and scanner) and there is never any mess to clear up afterwards.

Technology know-how

For digital scrapbooking, you will need a relatively new computer with plenty of storage and memory, a CD or DVD burner or an external hard drive (see pages 170-1) and a colour printer. A scanner is very useful, but not essential, especially if you already own a digital camera. In terms of memory, your computer will need to have sufficient RAM (Random Access Memory) – think of it as 'brain power'– to ensure fast performance, giving you the option of doing different things at the same time without your computer slowing down or 'crashing'. You will also need a large amount of storage space (also referred to as memory) on your actual hard drive, in the form of MB (megabytes) or GB (gigabytes) on which to save your current layout documents.

Selecting software

When choosing which software program to buy, first consider (along with the cost) what you are likely to want to do with it. If you plan to manipulate images and create your own elements and lettering, you will need a graphics package that offers these functions (see pages 162-3). If, however, you are only interested in producing layouts by organizing different elements upon the page, then a simpler layout or quick-page type program will be more appropriate (visit the websites on page 171 for more advice on programs).

must know

The internet is an incredible resource for the dedicated scrapbooker. Surf the net for scrapbooking-related websites and information, and use it to check out and download or order supplies and software (including a wealth of free stuff such as fonts and alphabets, digital images, embellishments, patterns and templates). See pages 186-8.

Preparing your photos

The growing popularity of digital cameras has contributed enormously to the increase in electronic scrapbooking, and many people are now well versed in downloading, printing and making basic corrections and changes to their digital images.

Photo editing

You may wish to keep your photo editing to just resizing or cropping your images, or enhancing your photos using an anti red-eye function, if you have one. Or you may enjoy manipulating your images and creatively altering them to suit your exact purposes. With the correct software and a little experience, you can quickly learn to retouch your photos, change colours, blend backgrounds, create special effects, such as neon, stained glass or charcoal, make patterned backgrounds, blend images, and add pop-out effects, blurs and smudges.

There are many photo editing programs available. The most popular of these are Adobe Photoshop,

Adding a blurring effect behind the central image gives the impression of movement.

Photoshop Elements (similar to Photoshop but with fewer functions and comes free with many scanners and printers), Jasc Paint Shop Pro, Digital Image Suite and Corel Draw. Some software is available by download as trial or demo versions. Experiment with different ones to see which works best for you. To help you there are many tutorials available online – some are free, some may require payment, and some even provide you with digital elements that you can download to use in your designs.

Starting out

You can use your photo editor to work on pictures that you have taken digitally or scanned (see pages 90–1). Simply choose your photos and open them from within your graphics program. You can even include stock or library photos in your layouts. These are available from the internet on CD or they can be downloaded (type 'stock photos' in your internet search engine for the sites), but beware of copyright infringements as many of these may be available for personal use but not for sharing or for posting online.

Digital photo formats

Photos and digital elements can be saved in different formats, usually TIFF (tag image file format), which are large files where more of the detail has been preserved, or jpeg (joint photographic expert group), which are smaller files but still of good quality. Other types of image files include png (portable network graphics) or gif (graphic interchange format), which are very popular with web designers, as they provide good quality images in small sized files, but are not usually of high enough quality for printed material.

must know

Never edit, change or manipulate the originals of any scans or digital photos; always make copies first and store your original images somewhere safe. You might even like to archive them in a 'master images' folder created especially for this purpose.

Scanning and printing

Scanners and printers are invaluable scrapbooking tools, but you need to make sure that you know how to use your equipment properly to get the best results each time.

Getting to know your tools

Scanners and printers all have basic or default settings to make them easy to use. However, taking the time to find out all the different functions available and learning what the various settings do will greatly improve the images you can produce. For example, selecting the appropriate paper setting (glossy, matte, photo) on your printer will produce a much better image.

Resolution (ppi vs dpi)

To ensure good quality pages, you will need to know a little about 'resolution' when scanning and printing. Essentially, resolution refers to the level of detail or clarity of an image: the higher the resolution

As an alternative to using commercial digital background papers, scan your own images and use them as backgrounds instead. Create background papers that are specific to your design, as in the snow scene shown here.

the more detail there will be in your image. Logically, this also results in a larger image file. For digital cameras, computers and scanners, resolution is usually measured in ppi (the number of 'pixels per inch' that the image contains; 'pixel' referring to the number of 'picture elements' – rather like the tiny tiles in a mosaic – contained within the image), whereas for printers it is measured in dpi (the number of 'dots per inch' that the device is capable of printing, see pages 90–1).

For printed material, 300 dpi is considered to be the industry standard, as the human eye cannot really perceive quality levels greater than this. If you also want to email or share your layouts online, you will need to create a copy, which you can save as a jpeg. The setting can be changed to 72 dpi and you can reduce the overall image size to make the file even smaller.

Scanning and printing tips

When resizing images, be aware of resolution. Enlarging any image in your layout will result in loss of quality, which means that if you double the size of any image the quality will be half as good. One way around this is to scan your images at larger sizes in the first place.

When scanning 'lumpy' items or layouts, be careful to prevent any shadows creeping into the scan. Make sure that the room is dark to reduce the amount of light that can seep in under the scanner cover.

You will only be able to print layouts to the paper width of your printer. For larger formats you will need to take your layout to a printing bureau or copy shop or, if you regularly need to print to a larger size, you might consider investing in a new printer.

must know

There are numerous scrapbooking websites where you can post (upload) your designs publicly, either just for fun or to get feedback on your work. There are also forums where you can ask for advice or share experiences with other scrappers. See pages 186–8 for just a few of the many websites available.

Creating pages and layouts

Digital scrapbooking has two main strands to it – creating and editing your images and other digital elements, and importing the different elements into your layout to create your page.

Getting started

To create your digital scrapbooking page you will need software that can manipulate graphics and text. Many scrapbookers use the photo-editing programs mentioned on pages 162–3, but there are simpler ones that have been developed especially for scrapbookers, such as Scrapbook Factory Deluxe or iRemember (use your search engine to find these on the internet).

There are also 'freebie' digital kits available online to give you a feel for working digitally (for example, see www.cottagearts.net). There are sometimes samples offered by companies that also sell a range of downloadable scrapbooking products and resources (see pages 186–8). They include background papers, lettering and digital elements such as tags, ribbons and other embellishments that can be imported into your graphics software or layout programme.

The basics of digital page layout

Ultimately, what you are able to create within your digital environment will be partly dependent on the software you have chosen and partly upon your level of skill in using it. When crafting your designs, depending on your actual software, you will usually create layers of digital background papers, photos and other elements to build your page in much the same way as you would if you were making a conventional paper layout.

First, you will need to open a new file (choosing your page size – usually A4 or 12in x 12in [30.48cm x 30.48cm]). Next, select your background colour, then add more and more layers using digital papers, photos and other digital elements. You can either open your digital images and copy and paste each one into a new layer, or simply import or drag them if this function is available in your particular program. Use the appropriate 'tools' to slide or move, resize, grab, drag or copy and paste your items into position. If in doubt, use the software 'Help' menu.

Alternatively, if you are working into a layout program that provides you with a page kit template, you will simply copy, import or drag the various items into the spaces provided.

Kit templates leave spaces into which you drop your own photos and also provide you with various embellishments – like this leaf motif – to enhance your design.

1 The boy has been cut out from a copy of the original photo and saved to be put into another image (above).

2 Depending on your software, use layers to place the digital cutout onto a new background (right).

Fonts, colours and extras

Putting the final touches to digital layouts is a dream, especially when it comes to adding text and titles, as there are endless fonts and effects to choose from, and text can be coloured, resized and rotated at the click of a button.

must know

A 'scraplift' is when you take something from another layout and use it as inspiration for your own. Use sketches to inspire you by simply arranging your items on the page in roughly the same positioning as shown in the sketch (see kiwiscraps.com or scrap-maps.com). Or base your design upon someone else's layout, but don't forget to add your own special touch or to acknowledge them, particularly if you are posting your final page layout online.

Adding text

Creating digital journalling, captions and titles is incredibly easy, as text can be manipulated in any way you choose, depending on the flexibility of your software. You may even have the option of warping, creating a bevelled effect or even flipping it to create a mirror image. Titles can also be created by using alphabet sets. Alphabet letters are images, not fonts, and need to be imported or dropped into your layouts in the same way as you would with other images, building your words letter by letter. Type in 'digital scrapbooking alphabet' in your search engine to find out where to get these.

Using colours

One important consideration when producing digital layouts is to ensure that your text will be legible over the background colour you have selected. This is particularly key if you are planning on sharing your digital layouts online.

One of the best ways of doing this is to use a high contrast between the background colour and the text itself. Extremes of light and dark work very well, black and white being the most extreme of all. Another good way of achieving this is by contrasting warm and cold colours. But bear in mind that cold

colours appear to be further away from you, while warm colours appear to be closer (see page 102). Hence, it is best to choose warmer colours for text or illustrations and colder colours for backgrounds.

Colours have a natural order and it is advisable to stay within that. Yellow is considered to be 'naturally' lighter than blue. Therefore, using a colour scheme that uses a dark yellow and a pale blue will feel uncomfortable. Using bright yellow lettering on a darker shade of blue will be much more satisfactory. Black on white, yellow on blue or black, and blue on white are all highly legible. Green on red is hard to read and should be avoided.

Titles and lettering can be created digitally by typing in text using different fonts or created with digital alphabet sets.

Finishing touches

To give the illusion of depth and make your page look more realistic, a useful effect is to add 'drop shadows'. This produces the illusion of a shadow around your item (image or lettering), creating a slightly three-dimensional effect. Most graphics or photo-editing software will include this as an option under the 'Effects' or 'Styles' menu.

If you are creating a webpage from your designs and are feeling adventurous, don't forget that you can always add extras such as sounds and short video clips or even animations into your designs.

You can create a raised, bevelled effect to your lettering using your chosen software package.

How to use digital pages

Once you have created your digital scrapbooking pages, you have a choice of what to do next. You can either print them out and treat them as traditional paper layouts, store them on your computer, send them to friends and family via email, or post them on a website and share them online.

Digital display

Sending your scrapbooking pages via email or posting them online are perfect ways of sharing your digital designs.

Some scrapbookers simply keep copies of digital pages on computer, sometimes using them as screensavers or wallpaper, or displaying them as a

'slideshow' album. Others create their pages and albums using traditional methods, but then scan or photograph them as a means of preserving or displaying them.

Digital pages can be sent as email attachments to share with others, or they can be shared online by uploading them onto personal website or dedicated scrapbooking online galleries.

Documents that contain a number of images tend to be large in size, so you will also need to create a smaller version to send via email or post online. This can be done by reducing the size of the document itself and by saving it as a jpeg (or jpg) instead of a tiff file. If you own a copy of Adobe Acrobat, you can create a pdf (portable document format) which can be viewed by anyone with Acrobat Reader. (This software can be downloaded free from www.adobe.com).

Saving and storing

Whether your pages are made by traditional paper methods or created digitally, regular scrapbooking albums remain a popular way of displaying your designs. With digital pages, however, you are not limited to only one copy: once you have generated your page you can print out multiple copies for family and friends. Digital versions can also be reprinted if the original print becomes damaged or discoloured. (You can also scan or photograph your paper layout to create a digital image for archiving purposes and printing extra copies, as well.) Always print on photo-quality paper for best colour reproduction (see page 90), either glossy finish or matte, as you prefer. If you are not happy with the quality of your home printer, take your files to be processed at a copy bureau or print shop.

want to know more?

- Choosing lettering 50-1
- Using colour 42-3
- Using digital photographs 90-1
- Basic cropping 68-9
- Sections and segments 80-3
- Journalling 136-7
- Project ideas 140-1
- Simple optical illusions 150-1
- Photo montage 152-3

weblinks

- amsdigiscraps.com
- cottagearts.net
- fxfoto.com
- scrapbook.com
- scrapbookmax.com
- scrapbook-bytes.com
- scrapgirls.com
- scraptutor.com
- shortcourses.com
- ukscrappers.co.uk

8 Special occasions

Celebrations and festivities provide the ultimate opportunity for special scrapbooking designs. Choose colours, styles and materials that reflect something of the quality of the occasion itself, adding to the tone that you wish to portray. But never forget that the most important element of many scrapbooking pages, particularly when it comes to major events or celebratory occasions, will be the photographs. So, when planning projects for particularly memorable events, let yourself be guided and inspired by the content of the photographs themselves.

High days and holidays

Festive occasions may have associations with particular colours, objects or themes, and considering these can be helpful when planning your design. However, study your photographs carefully and be led by them when making your final choices.

Colour schemes and key features

It might be that your choice of picture(s) leads you to conclude that an 'alternative' colour scheme is appropriate, rather than a design based on traditional colours and visual associations. In the project featured opposite, the blue of the Santa illustration has been used as the main inspiration for the colour scheme, as opposed to traditional red and green Christmas colours. A complementary background blue has been selected to represent a clear winter sky, and this is the dominant feature of the design.

A seasonal effect can be achieved by basing a design upon a grid divided into thirds (see page 37), so that different elements which are representative of the season in question can be strongly defined in the background. In the sample layout shown, the winter sky takes up the top two-thirds, while the hills (which are cut out from textured white card decorated with silver glitter), fill the final third.

Adding embellishments to your design can emphasize the particular theme of your layout and reinforce the message you are trying to convey. In the example shown, the punched-out snowflakes and trees and foliage on the snow-covered hills both create an unmistakably wintry feel. The use of Christmassy colours punctuates the seasonal theme still further.

must know

To make shaker boxes like the one featured in the design on the opposite page, you can either use foam mounts (squares or strips) to fasten the acetate 'window' to the base or, for a flatter option, simply fix it in place with double-sided tape and place a cardboard frame over the top to hide the glued edges. (See also pages 132-5.)

The simple cut-and-torn paper landscape provides a
delightful background to the colourful and amusing central
image of Santa in his spaceship with boy-Rudolph!

Mixing paper types

Using papers of various shades and textures can turn a simple design into something quite dazzling. The Halloween project on pages 178–9 uses a different paper for each segment of the pumpkin, a technique that can be used in virtually any layout. The pumpkin featured in this layout was created by cutting a panel from each paper and piecing them all together. Cut the eyes and mouth out of black paper and paste them on top: if you use the same paper as for your background they will look as if they have been cut into the pumpkin.

Finding patterns

As well as drawing objects and items freehand (such as a pumpkin), look in books and magazines for inspiration. Children's colouring books can be an invaluable source of simple, useful ideas. If you have internet access, it is worthwhile searching online for downloadable items (many of which may be available at no cost).

Razzle dazzle

The large, glittery lettering is perfect for a playful and colourful layout such as this. It matches the style of the rest of the piece and is in keeping with the huge pumpkin on the left-hand page, giving a sense of balance to the design. The shiny red decorative spirals reflect the colour and feel of the title lettering.

watch out!

Make sure that the maximum amount of glitter sticks to the glue by placing a piece of clean paper over the top of your lettering and pressing gently with a soft cloth. When cleaning up your glitter lettering, let the glue dry fully before brushing excess glitter away.

1 Using a soft pencil, either trace (see page 87) or draw your design freehand onto a piece of tracing paper. Place the tracing face down onto the reverse side of the colour paper and scribble over the back to transfer your design onto the colour paper.

2 Glue pens are excellent for creating unusual lettering or designs. Practise on a piece of scrap, then either work freehand or mark out your design to follow in pencil (or white crayon).

3 Liberally scatter glitter over the top of your glue. Leave to set, then shake away the excess glitter. Brush gently with a soft paintbrush to remove any remaining loose flakes.

must know

For designs that run over two pages, avoid positioning any photos or images across the centrefold of your layout. If this is not possible, make sure that the centre line does not cut through any of your subjects' faces. In our example the mid-line cuts through the ghost-child's sheet, but does not touch his face, although, in this instance, it is slightly less important as we cannot actually see his real features.

Composition

This layout provides an example of the interesting tricks you can play with composition. To create something similar, choose images with clear outlines and cut into silhouettes. Don't worry if they are at different scales, as this will make the composition of your design more unusual and eye-catching.

Choose an appropriate place for your silhouetted images on the page by positioning them around your focal point (in this case, the giant pumpkin); they

could be sitting on the ground, leaning or even standing on top of it.

You can add to your design by using torn shapes in contrasting colours, such as the black and white ghosts shown below. The inclusion of fantasy characters adds an extra dimension and, in the example shown, a touch of the supernatural. The use of both positive and negative versions of torn shapes (see page 62) is the key here, reinforced by adding a torn-edge red mount behind the white ghost to pick the shape out even more strongly from the background.

'Googly' eyes are fun to use and full of character. Fix them into place with mini glue dots or tiny pieces of double-sided tape; liquid glue is likely to be too messy for this purpose.

Celebrations

A wedding in the family means you can have fun finding creative ways of preserving your memories of the big day. Make some special layouts to commemorate this most memorable of events.

Champagne moments

For that extra-special occasion, design a layout which fizzes with visual impact and yells 'celebration'.

To create a design using sumptuous speciality papers like the one below, try selecting card in two tones to create a neutral yet elegant background. This layout was enhanced by adding rich Indian papers to decorate the large paper cutout bottle, the main focal

A selection of speciality papers were cut from a bottle-shaped template and pieced together to make this realistic bottle design.

point of the design. The champagne glasses were made from two layers of vellum, each cut to a hand-drawn template – one slightly smaller than the other – and stuck together to create a 3D effect. These are also decorated with ribbon from one of the wedding gifts.

Vellum is delicate and buckles easily, so it needs to be cut with great care. It is also essential to use invisible adhesive when working with this material, as anything else would show through and could ruin your design.

In the sample layout shown, the champagne theme has been further developed by cropping the photos themselves into 'champagne bubble' circles. These are of different sizes and have been arranged on the page with vellum bubbles, cut in similar sizes, to add texture to the design and provide a layering effect.

must know
The finishing touches to this project that lift the page and help the whole design come alive are the little glitter 'bubbles'. You will often find that your page can be completely transformed by the addition of one tiny detail.

Occasions to remember

Really special events deserve good quality, tasteful materials and elegant typefaces which are in perfect keeping with the tone and atmosphere of your subject matter.

Extra special silhouetting

The use of 3D silhouettes emphasizes the key elements of layouts inspired by special occasions and gives them an impression of quality which will set them apart.

To really lift your design and draw extra focus to a photograph, start by making a copy of the original picture and enlarging it by 20 per cent. Cut a complete silhouette of the central figure(s) from the larger copy and fix it to the partial silhouette of the original version. Use tiny foam mounting squares to fix the silhouette in place, in order to give the image a slightly 3D feel and make it stand out more strongly

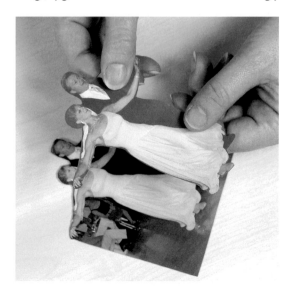

Fix foam squares to the back of the upper silhouette, rather than to the background photo. This eliminates the risk of any of the adhesive squares being visible around the edge of the cutout.

The see-through quality of the vellum alters its effect slightly, depending on the surface behind it. Always use invisible adhesive to fix vellum, to avoid the risk of staining and show-through.

than a standard silhouette. The layout featured on these pages demonstrates this effect very well.

To set off your 3D silhouettes to their best effect, select a decorated paper – like for instance the stripy-patterned one used here – to create a dramatic background and provide the perfect stage for your figure(s). Enhance the background by using vellum for your lettering and title panels and perhaps rubber stamp designs and decorated strips like those included above, for added interest.

A touch of class

Silver or gold highlights are the perfect choice for memorable events and anniversaries, lending a note of sophistication and elegance. Make panels, hearts and stars from a mixture of plain- and textured-finish silver card, using a corner-rounder punch to soften any sharp corners. To finish, echo the silver theme by adding delicate jewels to each corner of the title and lettering panels.

want to know more?

- Adding texture 44-7
- Adding accessories 52-5
- Techniques for extra effects 60-3
- Silhouettes and shadows 98-101
- Making fold outs 132-5
- 3D illusions 148-9

weblinks

- lifetimemoments.com
- scrapmagic.com
- deco-pages.com
- pagesoftheheart.net

Need to know more?

Books are an extremely valuable resource as a means of improving your techniques, allowing you to learn and develop new skills, keeping you in touch with the latest tools, materials and products and supplying you with an endless source of inspiration and ideas.

Further reading

Altered books

Bode Smiley, Jan, *Altered Board Book Basics and Beyond: For Creative Scrapbooks, Altered Books and Artful Journals* (C&T Publishing, 2005)

Frye Hauer, Pamela , Ghumm, Erikia, *Montage Memories: Creating Altered Scrapbook Pages* (Memory Makers Books, 2004)

Mason, Jennifer, *Pockets, Pull-outs, and Hiding Places: Interactive Elements for Altered Books, Memory Art, and Collage* (Quarry Books, 2005)

Creative techniques

Creative Paper Techniques for Scrapbooks (Memory Makers Books, 2002)

Curry, Nancy, *Texture Effects for Rubber Stamping* (North Light Books, 2004)

Davis, Dee , Cooper, Gail B, *The Victorian Scrap Gallery: A Collection of over 500 Full-Color Victorian-Era Images* (Watson-Guptill Publications, 2003)

Harrison, Holly, Atkinson, Jennifer, Grasdal, Paula, *Collage Sourcebook: Exploring the Art and Techniques of Collage* (Quarry Books, 2005)

Hellmuth, Claudine, *Collage Discovery Workshop: Beyond the Unexpected* (North Light Books, 2005)

Jenkins, Alison, *Absolute Beginner's Decoupage: The Simple Step-by-Step Guide to Creating Beautiful Decoupage* (Watson-Guptill Publications, 1999)

Johnson, Robin, *Designing with Vellum* (Dan Maryon Leisure Arts, 2005)

McGraw, Maryjo, *Creative Rubber Stamping Techniques* (North Light Books, 1998)

Miller, Jill, *Special Effects Scrapbooking: Creative Techniques for Scrapbookers at All Levels* (Watson-Guptill, 2003)

Digital scrapping

Hook, Patrick, *Need to know? Digital Photography* (Collins, 2006)

Martin, Sue, *Digital Delights for Scrapbooking* (C & T Publishing, 2006)

Murray, Katherine, *Creative Digital Scrapbooking: Designing Keepsakes on Your Computer* (Peachpit Press, 2004)

Rose, Carla, *Digital Memories: Scrapbooking with Your Computer* (Que, 2004)

Warner, Janine, *Digital Family Album Basics* (Amphoto Books, 2006)
Wines-Reed, Jeanne, Wines, Joan, *Digital Scrapbooking For Dummies* (2005)

Journalling and lettering
Diehn, Gwen, *The Decorated Journal: Creating Beautifully Expressive Journal Pages* (Lark Books, 2006)
Higgins, Becky, McGowan, Siobhan, *The Art of Creative Lettering: 50 Amazing New Alphabets You Can Make for Scrapbooks, Cards, Invitations, and Signs* (Porch Swing Publishing, 1999)
Scrapbook Journaling Made Simple: Tips for Telling the Stories Behind Your Photos (Memory Makers Books, 2002)

Scrapbooking, general
Aitman, Joy, *Start Scrapbooking* (Search Press, 2005)
Budget Scrapbooking (Memory Makers Books, 2005)
Carter, Rebecca, et al, *The Ultimate Scrapbooking Book* (Sterling, 2001)
Carter, Rebecca, *Scrapbooking for the First Time* (Sterling, 1999)
Complete Book of Creative Scrapbooking, The (Murdoch Books, 2005)
Edwards, Ali, *A Designer's Eye for Scrapbooking* (PriMedia Scrapbooking, 2004)
Gerbrandt, Michele, *Mastering Scrapbook Page Design* (Memory Makers, 2004)
Gerbrandt, Michele and Arquette, Kerry,

Scrapbooking with Memory Makers (Hugh Lauter Levin Associates, 1999)
Klassen, Pam, *Making Gift Scrapbooks in a Snap* (Memory Makers Books, 2004)
McKenna, Sarah, *Cropping for Scrapbooks* (Search Press, 2005)
More Quick & Easy Scrapbook Pages (Memory Makers Books, 2005)
Pedersen, A, *The Book of Me: A Guide to Scrapbooking about Yourself* (EFG, 2002)
Pickering Rothamel, Susan, *The Encyclopedia of Scrapbooking Tools & Techniques* (Sterling/Chapelle, 2005)
Riddell, Louise, *The Complete Book of Scrapbooking: Projects and Techniques* (Thunder Bay, 2004)
Scrapbooking Your Favorite Family Memories (Memory Makers Books, 2003)
White, Tracy (ed), *Creating Keepsakes' Encyclopedia of Scrapbooking* (Leisure Arts, 2005)
Wolmarans, Annamè, *Create Your Own Scrapbook* (Struik Publishers, 2005)

Photography
Bearnson, Lisa, McGowan, Siobhan *Mom's Little Book of Photo Tips* (Creating Keepsakes Books, 1999)
Tyler Jones, Allison, *Designing With Photos* (Leisure Arts, 2005)
Zielske, Cathy, *Clean and Simple Designs for Scrapbooking: Ideas for Design, Photography, Journaling & Typography* (Primedia Scrapbooking, 2004)

Useful websites

The internet is an ever-expanding goldmine for the scrapbooker, providing an invaluable source for supplies and materials, downloads and information and some even offer free items, ranging from fonts to printable patterns and page accents.

Clipart and graphics

www.best-of-clipart.com
www.clip-art.com
www.clipsahoy.com
www.coolclipart.com
www.creativehomeartsclub.com
www.cutecolors.com
www.free-clip-art.com
www.free-graphics.net
www.scrapbookgraphics.com

Digital scrapbooking

www.computerscrapbook.com
www.digitaljuice.com
www.digitalscrapbookplace.com
www.escrappers.com
www.scrapaddict.com
www.scrapbookmax.com
www.scrapgirls.com
www.shabbyprincess.com
www.twopeasinabucket.com

Fonts

www.1001fonts.com
www.dafont.com
www.fontgarden.com
www.itcfonts.com
www.larabiefonts.com
www.onescrappysite.com
www.fontconnection.com
www.momscorner4kids.com/fonts
www.myfonts.com

Freeware and shareware

www.bisous.biz/scrap/scrap_freebee.htm
www.cottagearts.net
www.craftfreebies.com
www.creativity-portal.com
www.freebiedot.com
www.freeserifsoftware.com
www.red-castle.com
www.scrapmagic.com

Galleries, forums, resources and online shopping

www.3scrapateers.com
www.sevengypsies.com
www.apeekintoyesterday.com
www.bluebazaar.com.au
www.boxerscrapbooks.com
www.cottagearts.net
www.croppinparadise.com

www.downmemorylaneco.com
www.kindredcreations.com
www.lastingimpressions.com
www.magicscraps.com
www.outside the margins.com
www.paperwishes.com
www.pebblesinmypocket.com
www.scrap2gether.com
www.scrapbook.com
www.scrappingwithstyle.com
www.scrapbooksandmore.com.au
www.scrapjazz.com
www.thedigichick.com
www.twopeasinabucket.com

Patterns, templates, accents and extras

www.canon.com/c-park
www.cropycats.com
www.deco-pages.com
www.disney-clipart.com
www.bydonovan.com/templates.html
www.matterofscrap.com
www.primdoodles.com/printables.asp
www.primgraphics.com
www.scrapbookscrapbook.com
www.raggedyscrappin.com
www.scrapbookersparadise.com
www.scrapping-place.com
www.thelittlepillow.com/albumpgdl.html

Products and supplies

www.acherryontop.com/
www.addictedtoscrapbooking.com

www.allaboutscrapbooking.com
www.artaccents.net
www.chatterboxinc.com
www.clearsnap.com
www.closetomyheart.com
www.clubscrap.com
www.crazyscraps.com
www.creativememories.com
www.designerdigitals.com
www.emaginationcrafts.com
www.fiberscraps.com
www.heritagescrapbooks.com
www.hobbycraft.co.uk
www.justamemory.com
www.kalulu.com
www.ktcrafts.com
www.makingmemories.com
www.paperaddict.com
www.paperstyle.com
www.runningrhino.com
www.scraparts.com
www.scrapbookclearance.com
www.scrapbookexpress.com
www.scrapbooks.com
www.scrapgal.com
www.scraplove.com
www.scrapmagic.com
www.scrappindreams.com
www.scrappycatcreations.com
www.scrapworks.com
www.thescrapstop.com
www.tollitandharvey.co.uk
www.thevintageworkshop.com
www.twiddleys.co.uk

www.uptowndesign.com
www.windowsoftime.com
www.wishinthewind.com

Online learning

www.3scrapateers.com
http://beginnersguide.com/
   arts-crafts
http://beginnersguide.com/
   arts-crafts/digital-scrapbooking
www.cottagearts.net/tutorials
www.officeteacher.com
www.scrapbook-elements.com/tutorials
www.scrapboxx.com.au
www.scraptutor.com

Quotes and phrases

www.bartelby.com
www.brainyquote.com
www.quotemountain.com
www.saidwhat.co.uk
www.scrapoetry.com
www.thequotegarden.com
http://en.thinkexist.com

Scrapbooking crops, communities, articles, tutorials and downloads

http://scrapbooking.about.com
www.columbusscrappers.org
www.cropperscottage.com
www.digiscrapdivas.com
www.homeandfamilynetwork.com/
   crafts/scrap.html

www.madcropper.com
www.pagesoftheheart.net
www.rakscraps.com
www.scrapbook-bytes.com
www.scrapbookersplayground.com
www.scrapbooking101.net
www.scrapfairy.blogspot.com
www.scrapfriends.us
www.scrapjazz.com/topics/techniques
www.scrapo.com
www.scrapvillage.com
www.scribblesonline.com
www.ukscrappers.co.uk

Software: downloads and information

www.adobe.com
www.corel.com
www.microsoft.com
www.hewlettpackard.com
www.jasc.com
www.kodak.com
www.macscrapbook.com
www.ulead.com

Top sites and links

www.justamemory.com
www.lovetoknow.com
www.scrapbookingtop50.com
www.scrapbookingtop50.com.au/
   topsites
www.scrapbookingtop50.com.au/
   digitaltopsites
www.scraplink.com

Index

Acknowledgements

The author and publishers would like to thank Nick Parry at Tollit & Harvey (www.tollitandharvey.co.uk) and Helen Morris at The Stencil Library (www.stencil-library.com) for their help and support in providing materials for projects. Special thanks also to Lorraine Wheeler at www.justamemory.com for her help in providing layouts, and to Kerenza Swift and Ione Walder for their cover artwork.

We would also like to thank the following websites for their invaluable contributions: www.amsdigiscraps.com, www.ingriddijkers.com, www.inkredible.com, www.kalulu.com, www.lovebugscrapbooking.com, www.noreimerreason.com, www.nw4you.com, www.scrapbook.com.

○ **Collins** need to know?

Look out for these recent titles in Collins' practical and accessible need to know? series.

Other titles in the series: